A Weekly Encounter

A Weekly Encounter

Fifty-Two Meditations of Hope

Dr. Erwin K. Thomas

ISBN: 1517351472
ISBN 13: 9781517351472

To my loving wife, Mary; son, Matthew;
and daughter-in-law, Shannon

Contents

Acknowledgments

THIS BOOK STARTED out as diary of personal meditations. Soon it took on a life of its own and I began worshiping at a number of churches in Virginia Beach to gain greater insights into the Word of God. Over a twenty-four-month period I attended Mass at St. Gregory the Great Catholic Church, Saint Matthew's Catholic Church, Church of the Holy Family Catholic Church, Church of the Ascension Catholic Church, Kempsville Presbyterian Church, and Rock Church International. But I am presently back with the Church of the Holy Apostles—an ecumenical congregation of Episcopalians and Roman Catholics.

I was most grateful for the experiences that these churches offered by their preaching, music and other ministries. Because of a desire to conduct further exploration of prayer, I began going to these churches' bazaars and thrift stores, like Goodwill, CHKD, and the Salvation Army Hampton Roads, looking for used Christian books.

Happily, I made excellent discoveries of books on the Christian faith, many of which I have included in the Selected Readings section of this book. To complement these resources, I searched on eBay, Amazon, and at Barnes & Noble bookstores. As a rule, I would often visit Central and Kempsville libraries to compose and reflect on these meditations; blog them at Blogger; and post them on the social media sites Google +, Facebook and Twitter. I was appreciative of the feedback I was getting from these sites.

Most of the quotations used from famous and world-renowned personalities were those found mainly on the Internet sites of BrainyQuote and Goodreads. These sites are replete with quotes and it was at times challenging to figure out which ones to use in a meditation.

I cannot stress enough how my wife, Mary of forty-five years encouraged me in this publishing venture. She is my soul mate, good friend, and was always present for me to run my ideas by. My son, Matthew, advised me on filing and other matters concerning this project. Moreover I wish to thank Christine Tate for being a resource person. I would also like to thank all the authors I met last June at the 2015 Christian Authors Festival at the Meyera Oberndorf Central Library, Virginia Beach, Virginia, for guiding me to publish this book with Amazon's CreateSpace. Lastly, I sincerely wish to thank Michelle, CreateSpace Editor, for the great job in editing this manuscript.

Erwin K. Thomas, PhD

Introduction

THIS BOOK OF fifty-two meditations grew out of my desire to "live by the Spirit, I say, and do not gratify the desires of the flesh." (Galatians 5:16 NRSV). My main concern was to focus on the hope promised us by our Lord and Savior, Jesus Christ. Hence the title: *A Weekly Encounter: Fifty-Two Meditations of Hope*. It's hopeful for there is the message of Jesus Christ's resurrection and salvation throughout its pages.

Like other devotional books, this one not only quotes over fifty biblical passages, but also focuses on quotes drawn from BrainyQuotes, Goodreads and the *Dictionary of Quotations* to enhance the essays on these meditations.

Many of quotes used were said by famous and world-renowned personalities, such as Thomas Jefferson (1743–1826), Eleanor Roosevelt (1884–1962), William Shakespeare (1564–1616), John F. Kennedy (1917–1963), Pope Francis (b. 1936), Martin Luther King, Jr. (1929–1968), Mother Teresa (1910–1997), Mahatma Gandhi (1869–1948), Billy Graham (b. 1918), Desmond Tutu (b. 1931), Aristotle (384–322 BC), Voltaire (1694–1778), Confucius (551–479 BC), and many more. These individuals are from diverse cultures, national origins, and creeds have spanned the ages.

It was interesting to find that some secular and non secular leaders often meditated on the magnanimity of their Creator. My objective therefore was to work their sayings into the basic teachings of scripture and provide a Thought of the Week in Bible verses.

It is hoped that a reader may focus each week on one of these fifty-two entries, or spend much more time on a single meditation. Each week's meditation is generally broken down into smaller meditations that are relevant to the main meditation discussed.

In pondering *Fifty-Two Meditations of Hope*, a reader may find comfort in the following three helpful questions:

1) What is your overall reaction to the meditation?
2) Did the quotes in the meditation shed light on its contents?
3) Did you find the meditation helpful?

At the conclusion of all fifty-two weekly entries, a reader may now answer a fourth question: Finally, in the author's message was it clear that there was overall hope for redemption and salvation?

Although the meditations are organized into various chapters, it is not necessary to read each in its proper sequence. A reader, if he or she likes, may choose to skip around and read what appeals to him or her on any particular week. Some may want to concentrate on a chapter at a time, while the more ambitious may read through the entire book of meditations in one sitting. What is important is that you do what is best and most convenient for you. You may even consider having a writing pad and pen handy to make notes as you explore and critique this book.

For more reading, I have carefully chosen books to include in the "Selected Readings" section for the further edification of readers. These are some of the more important Christian and non-Christian books I have read that have helped shape these meditations.

The Church

Authoritative Experiences

G OD IS THE ultimate for giving authoritative experiences. It's true that there has been a number of charismatic leaders, but for them to make an impact on society, they must be agents of the Living God. Some of these leaders have been blessed with charismatic anointing and they are divine officials. But to be truly authoritative depends solely on the grace of God. Most priests are such agents. They are known for their work and leading the worship services in the sanctuary. The Old and New Testaments are the foundation of those who have been blessed as being the rightful speakers of God. These individuals have all been anointed of the spirit.

Billy Graham (b. 1918), an American evangelical Christian who was ordained as a Southern Baptist minister observed, "The highest form of worship is the worship of the unselfish Christian service. The greatest form of praise is the sound of consecrated feet seeking out the lost and helpless." Graham touched on the way for those with authoritative experiences—to be of service.

Experiences of Inspiration

Some Christians have experienced the thrilling effects of divine power that fell on them. These are a rather compelling inspiration that has moved them to testify about the wonders of Christ. Those with contemplative spirits attest to this truth. For pulling down strongholds of wickedness, they use prayer as a weapon of the spirit. These individuals are generous, full of fervor and exemplify gifts of goodness, justice and peace.

Jensen Ackles (b. 1978), an American actor and director who is, known for his TV roles said, "What I enjoy most is the traveling to different places and meeting new people. For me, it's all about life experiences, and I'm very grateful that acting allows me so many interesting and fulfilling ones." Ackles finds inspiration through the different people he meets and experiences. Some of these people may strike him as simple and humble, and may teach him humility. Others may have personalities that exude confidence and their effect may well bolster his confidence in, for, and about people.

A Charismatic Prophet

For a charismatic prophet it's wonderful to be blessed with a spirit of ecstasy. Such a prophet will be known for his prophetic utterances—a life inspired by God's prophecies. It's a spiritual life with immense responsibilities, but the reward is great—profound spiritual joy and peace. To receive these rewards, one has to have the right spirit that touches lives and points them to the correct path with the authoritative Word of God. Elisabeth Kübler-Ross (1926–2004), a Swiss-American psychiatrist remarked, "I think that modern medicine has become like a prophet offering a life free of pain. It is nonsense. The only thing I know that truly heals people is unconditional love." For Kübler-Ross, a true prophet must show unconditional love in his actions.

Experiences of Divine Power

Albert Einstein (1879–1955), a German born theoretical physicist who developed the general theory of relativity was certain, "Great spirits have always encountered violent opposition from mediocre minds."

Truly great minds are known for their divine authentication. Some are blessed with the spirit of prophecy and serve exceptional spiritual food to believers and non believers alike. They are symbolic of a new spirit that has taken root in them. These individuals are the least among us, but they are still spiritually alert—quite animated and are greatly blessed.

Their sole objective is to present God's truth based on the Gospels. Moreover, they are living examples in our midst daily. Their works are most precious because they are done through their living God, the Provider, and Creator of all living and non living things.

Thought of the Week

"The Spirit of the Lord God is upon me; because the Lord hath anointed me to preach good tidings unto the meek...to proclaim liberty to the captives..."

—Isaiah 61:1 (KJV)

Meditation 2

Human Condition

What are perspectives on human lives? Humans can be noble and dignified; for these gifts, we're most grateful to God. However, we're fallen beings with rather distorted and corrupted natures. From birth, we were biologically tainted and have inherited a rather unreliable human condition. One such sin of this condition is racism, which has permeated our flesh. It was Jackie Robinson (1919–1972), the first African American Major League Baseball player who said, "I'm not concerned with your liking or disliking me … All I ask is that you respect me as a human being." To Robinson his thoughts about being human encompassed more than just racism.

God Created Man

About ten thousand years ago, God created man—a glorious act. Humankind was the pinnacle of his creative effort. People, by their very nature have a reflective awareness with ethical concerns. Throughout the ages, people have engaged in aesthetic endeavors and have a historical awareness. Humankind has witnessed great leaders and bad leaders who have ruled some powerful nations. People are also gifted with a metaphysical nature and have multiplied and exercised sovereignty over God's creation. Humans were created in God's image and have dominion over all other species on the earth. They are above all other creatures.

Alexandra Stoddard (b. 1941), an author, well-known interior designer and lifestyle philosopher expressed her happiness of the gifts that she has been blessed with. "Being a mother and grandmother is the best of the best of my life. My grandchildren multiply the joy my daughters bring me." Stoddard is very happy for these gifts of family of which she has been endowed by the Creator.

A Human as a Being
People are the apex of God's handiwork. They have anatomical similarities with many of God's creatures and they are well known for their language and tool-making culture. They are more than the "naked ape" and are undoubtedly gifts from God. People live with a shared responsibility—not only to their fellow human beings, but to all of God's creation. With God's personality, all of humankind also possesses a soul.

Jim Rohn (1930–2009), an American entrepreneur, author and motivational speaker known for his "rags to riches" story observed, "You must take personal responsibility. You cannot change the circumstances, the seasons, or the wind, but you can change yourself. That is something you have charge of." Rohn recognized that God gave us all a free will. As we grow older we learn how to make the best decisions. Real growth is not just physical, intellectual and emotional, but spiritual as well. For ultimate growth, Christians turn to Christ the arbiter and provider of all things.

Theory of Life
People are God-breathed. Within them is God's breath of life and they all have a living soul. There's always been a spirit-body connection. To put it another way, people are physical and non-physical beings. They have a physical

body, intellect, speech, a family and soul. A Christian knows this, for he or she practices brotherly love and looks forward to salvation. To him or her, life has no end because it's everlasting.

Oprah Winfrey (b. 1954), an American media proprietor and talk show host urged her audience to "breathe. Let go. And remind yourself that this very moment is the only one you know you have for sure."

Winfrey's remarks although relevant will bring her fans to the realization of their presence, but miss out on the fundamental promises in the Bible. In the present time, most can only think of a physical reality. But our future is physical and spiritual. In the Gospels, Christians are assured of an everlasting life. They have faith about what their future holds for them. The flesh passes away but the soul lives on and on. This experience is unlike any other, for Christians are assured that they will flourish in God's heavenly kingdom, where Jesus is seated at the Father's right hand. This is a certainty for which martyrs have sacrificed their lives by putting their trust in God. The faithful knows that there's a greater reality beyond the present time.

Thought of the Week
"So God created man in His own image, in the image of God created He him; male and female created He them.
    And God bless them…"

—Genesis 1:27–28 (KJV)

Meditation 3

People and Church
People go to church for many reasons, but there are bad and good reasons for doing so. It's good to follow the advice of Abbe Pierre (1912–2007), a former

French Catholic priest, and member of the resistance during World War II, who observed, "It's not enough to attend church and pray every Sunday; you have to act."

Poor Reasons

Some may say that they go to church because on Sundays their family always attends church. They simply follow in the footsteps of their family. It's their tradition. You hear it often said, "We grew up in the church so that's why we are in church." This doesn't make complete sense as the main reason for wanting to go to church.

There are those that say that although they were never faithful about church before, it's time to go. The reason they give is based on the fact that they ought to lay down roots. They will say that some churches won't marry them when it comes to tie the knot. Some older people believe that they have to be sure to be at a church that will bury them when they die. They may see this event as a dilemma to their family and friends if they aren't a member of a church. These may still be wrong reasons for going to church.

It doesn't matter which church persons attend, but if they do so for this next reason they will be out of place. I have heard it said, "If you want to meet a good Christian woman, find a church and you'll be sure to meet one. Just don't bother with the type that goes to nightclubs." Persons that say this, are also missing the main reasons of what a church is really about.

Good Reasons

Michele Bachmann (b. 1956), an American Republican and former member of the US House of Representatives from Minnesota's sixth Congressional district serves as a good example of a Christian upbringing. She stated, "I was born in a Christian family and brought up in a Lutheran church. My faith has been the center point of my life, since I was a child, but at sixteen years of age, I fully surrendered my life over to Christ. At that point, as a teenager, I began to grasp the concept of Christ's true love and forgiveness."

Some may not like Bachmann's politics, but it's wonderful to be introduced to church as a child. It doesn't matter which church it is, as long as it's truly Christian, and preaches the Word of God. As a new member you'll be baptized into the death and resurrection of Christ. The pastor will remind the members of the congregation that they are to help raise the children in their community as Christians.

As children grow up and become adolescents, their parents will see to it that they are confirmed. The pastor or bishop will lay hands on them. This rite indicates that they have attained the age of responsibility, and are mature enough to know the difference between right and wrong.

What Is Required?
As individuals grow in the faith tradition of their church—be it Catholic, Episcopal, Lutheran, Methodist, Presbyterian, or Baptist—they will attend Christian formation classes. They will come to realize that they have been blessed with a gift, or gifts, talents, and treasure, that they must share with their community.

Since these individuals are now part of the body of Christ, they will now endeavor to fulfill their special mission. Being older, they may discover that they have the gift of giving or teaching. As a result they may do more charitable work. These persons may work with manna, feeding the poor and homeless, collecting clothing for the underprivileged, and contributing to charitable organizations, such as a cancer society, diabetes association, or mental health groups, just to mention a few.

Having completed college and working at a job, they will tithe. These persons will meditate on the scriptures daily, attend a Bible study group, religious seminars, and be well prepared to take the next step in their life. After confirmation they have been receiving the sacrament of the Eucharist, but are now preparing for marriage. There's no problem, for through the church these individuals and their fiancees have been taking marriage counseling classes from their pastor. So when it comes time to be married, their groundwork is well laid. Once married, the couple may be blessed with children, they will have them baptized at their church and the cycle starts all over again.

In church they will all celebrate baptisms, confirmations, weddings, funerals and anniversaries. Their family's involvement in the community will be a living symbol to other members of their church and friends. They will have cultivated a variety of experiences through the life of their church and meet faithful and not so faithful members in their community. But through it all, they know that it's their calling to help build up the body of Christ.

Much older, their children are sure to find peace of mind. So when Dad or Mom becomes ill and dies, through their afflictions, they know that they can rest assured that there will be a fitting Mass at their church. Further, they are certain that once they exit from this earthly plane, they will enjoy everlasting life in heaven.

Thought of the Week
"And I will give you pastors according to Mine heart, which shall feed you with knowledge and understanding."

—Jeremiah 3:15 (KJV)

Meditation 4

Hidden Saints
Why must we look out for saints? It's because if we spot them we can discover unexpected blessings. Where do we find them? They are everywhere and we

may meet them while walking in the woods, shopping, in organizations, at churches, or when we just hop into a McDonald's or Hardee's to buy a cup of coffee. But how do know they are saints? We may be unable to recognize them because they appear as all sorts of people in different vocations. For one, when they greet you, you may be tempted to ignore them because they look quite ordinary.

Sometimes, they will strike up a conversation and you may not even realize that there is anything particularly striking or unusual about them. These saints may focus on some problem that you're concerned about and that you wish would go away. Then, here comes this man or woman and as he or she spoke with you, touched on the same matter that has been troubling you.

The matter may be whether you must quit your job for other work, financial problems or having a sick child at home. What can you do? You might have just relocated to a new town and are looking for an apartment. Then again, it may be that you simply wish to know the quickest way to your son's soccer game. This saint unexpectedly provided the answer you never imagined. You didn't realize it, but in hindsight you're sure that person with whom you were chatting, provided an answer that literally saved your life.

American singer-songwriter Bob Dylan (b. 1941), in his lyrics to the song "It's All Over Now, Baby Blue," sang about an orphan with his gun crying like a fire in the sun:

"Look out, the saints are coming through
And it's all over baby blue..."

Unlike the lines of these lyrics it's never over for saints because they are blessed with an eternal future. Saints pop up unexpectedly appearing in places and situations where you least expect to see them. During these times, they are working with and for us, helping to solve problems and shedding light on new ones.

Unexpected Saints

Some saints are considered hidden. On Vatican Radio on December 4th, 2014 Pope Francis (b. 1936), at morning Mass at Santa Marta recalled his experiences : "There are many hidden saints, men, women, fathers and mothers of families, sick people, priests who every day put into practice the love of Jesus; and this gives us hope."

By simply giving a cup of water to a thirsty beggar, a saint will be of help; this is just as important as feeding the starving in the midst of devastating earthquakes, hurricanes, tornadoes, floods, and droughts. You may see saints building homes for the homeless, digging wells in impoverished regions to bring fresh water, and relief, to villagers. While working in hospitals, medical centers and soup kitchens some still go unrecognized.

Throes of Life

In the throes of life, saints appear in places where there are severe pangs of pain and suffering. During extreme difficulties and troubles, they slave away with and for us. It may be an era of great revolutions or social change in the nations, but they are there with the down-trodden. In such agonizing crises they silently nurse wounds, caring for the dying, and sick.

Pop groups have sprung up capturing dark moments of life. The lyrics to the song "Throes of Perdition," by Trivium, use images of blind-folded and gagged people, firing squads, vultures and hyenas to promote themselves. Throes of Dawn, a band formed in 1994, is a dark-metal band from Finland whose music pushes the fear of pain in human existence. Their fare is emotional, dark and progressive, with growling, screaming and singing songs of bittersweet experiences. English rock band Pink Floyd, founded in 1979, and inducted into the US Rock and Roll Hall of Fame 1996, in their song "One of My Turns," sings:

"This is just a passing phase,
One of my bad days.

Would you want to watch TV?
Or get between the sheets?"

Although saints work globally, there are social deficiencies that still need attention. We find instances of these in pop culture, which is promoted worldwide.
But regardless of how bleak these situations are, the meek, hard working and
hidden saints are making a difference, by impacting communities for the better.

Thought of the Week
"Show us Thy mercy, O Lord, and grant us Thy salvation."

—Psalm 85:7 (KJV)

Meditation 5

Vision of Leadership
A vision of leadership calls for having a spirit of collegiality. Good leaders
know how to delegate and exercise legitimate power in the church. Inevitably,
they will summon the troops to pursue their long term plans. By so doing,
they are able to envision the relationships of the different committees they are
supervising. The leaders' insight will tell them how best to foster the actual-
ization of their flock. Through their direction their sheep will prosper and
be filled with inspiration to do their respective jobs. By the leaders' example,
they will be able to ignite the flame of the spirit of those under their direction
through the transformation of the environment.

American businessman Bo Bennett (b. 1972) stated, "Those who improve
with age embrace the power of personal growth and personal achievement and
begin to replace youth and wisdom, innocence and understanding, and lack
of purpose with self-actualization." Effective leaders will grow and guide their
flock in wisdom.

Ethical Leadership

Ethical leaders don't strive to control the group's creativity. They avoid the manipulation of the flock to get things done. Decisions aren't leader-centered but worker-centered. It's for them to be sure that they are understood and that their instructions are carried out. Their leadership is not dominant, but they set the example by their management style. Their noteworthy quality is being humble in serving others to work in unison with them, and their demeanor will show their ability to rally the work force.

It was a preeminent leader of India's independence movement, Mahatma Gandhi (1869-1948), who observed, "The best way to find yourself is to lose yourself in the service of others." This quality is what's expected of a leader. Pope Francis (b. 1936) remarked, "Every man, every woman who has to take up the service of government, must ask themselves two questions: 'Do I love my people in order to serve them better? Am I humble and do I listen to everybody, to diverse opinions in order to choose the best path?' If you don't ask these questions, your governance will not be good." These are questions a leader must answer in order to be accountable to their followers.

Peer Pressure

Leaders must resist psychological coercion. Their aim should be to strive for authentic personal fulfillment. Their approach with workers must not be lukewarm or heavy handed. At all cost they must avoid manipulating them to have the upper hand in decision making. All workers must be respected and honored for who they really are. Everyone must be treated like a colleague – and like the adults they really are. Benjamin Carson (b. 1951), an American author and retired neurosurgeon felt that, "no matter how good you are at planning, the pressure never goes away. So I don't fight it. I feed off it. I turn pressure into motivation to do my best." This ought to be an example of a leader who wishes to counter stress in a work environment.

Effective Communication

Leaders must be quick to listen. They must never look at themselves as desirous of increasing their status for personal gratification. Their foremost goal is to be a mediator of conflicts with their flock. They will practice authenticity and treat their supporters with the utmost respect and dignity. It is best for them to follow these guidelines on leadership that are spelled out in the scriptures. It'll be an exercise in spiritual growth by motivating their flock to higher levels of accomplishments. At no time must they give the appearance of being authoritarian. Such an approach will only damage a church's flock.

Quincy Adams (1767–1848), the sixth president of the United States and statesman was certain that, "if your actions inspire others to dream more, learn more, do more and become more, you are a leader." This ought to be the vision of every leader.

Thought of the Week
"He that is faithful in that which is least is faithful also in much: and he that is unjust in the least is unjust also in much."

—Luke 16:10 (KJV)

Meditation 6

Building Bridges
In life it's necessary to build bridges vertically and horizontally. A vertical bridge must be to God above—our heavenly Father. A horizontal one is made through loving our families, neighbors, friends and strangers. Jesus who is love died on a cross at Calvary for us. Let such love begin flowing from above and around us, for it unites and must be sustained. At its summit, it's creative and brings out the best in our broken and divided world. Its flame is indestructible, sweeping across nations and transforming cultures. It's inspirational to love and be loved. It's wonderful. Blessed are those that can love even their enemies and those who are a courageous and merciful lot. Love will never discriminate and Christians must learn to reach out passionately with love.

Elisabeth Elliot (b. 1926), a Christian author and speaker observed, "To be a follower of the Crucified means, sooner or later, a personal encounter with the cross. And the cross always entails loss. The great symbol of Christianity means sacrifice and no one who calls himself a Christian can evade this stark fact." True love is the cross and is an ideal bridge to spiritual maturity because Jesus showed us that where there's loss there's truly gain.

Inspire Hope
A bridge is love because it transports and inspires hope. It calls us to love all mankind while proclaiming the risen Christ. In doing so, a Christian is strengthened by the Holy Spirit—a fundamental basis of vertical hope. Hope like love has to be fervent and must be considered a lamp to be lit. It awakens justice for all, especially those who are marginalized in society. Every Christian is able to find their inspiration through the Bible, which speaks directly to the hearts. It was Brad Henry (b. 1963), a member of Democratic Party and the twenty-sixth governor of Oklahoma who felt that, "a good teacher can inspire hope, ignite the imagination, and instill a love of learning." Learning that's the foundation for progress in a country is a unique way of building a bridge of hope!

Father: Church's Pastor
It must always be remembered that the church is a missionary body. By its ministries, a pastor is constantly building bridges to his parishioners and the community, that reaches out to villages and towns around the globe. Much of this is brought about by the religious awakening of the flock. Parishioners and community workers are literally on fire for Christ when they serve others. In a believer's mind a biblical spirit lingers. Believers are humble folk that live according to the teachings of scripture. They proclaim the Word of God to those that hunger for justice. In witnessing, they acquire spiritual depth. These men and women are prudent in discernment and embrace pastoral challenges with vigor and enthusiasm. Much known for their charity, their presence extends to overpopulated slum areas of many cities. Robert C. Shannon (b. 1930), a retired preacher living in North Carolina expressed his gratitude for missionary work. He said, "Never pity missionaries; envy them. They are where the real action is—where life and death, sin and grace,

Heaven and Hell converge." Here Shannon points to attributes which are prominent with missionaries that we should aspire to. This is what is right to do.

Obstacles and Misunderstandings

Mother Teresa (1910–1997), a Roman Catholic religious sister and missionary in India commented, "Let us touch the dying, the poor, the lonely and the unwanted according to the graces we have received and let us not be ashamed or slow to do the humble work."

Christians must work with and anoint the poor and constantly dialogue with people from different cultures by seeking ways of bettering their circumstances. There ought to be more inter-religious meetings with believers of different faiths. No longer must the center seems as though it isn't a part of the whole. Osmosis between the center and the periphery must be promoted for all to become equally involved. Access to the sacraments has been a sticking point among some Christian denominations. Why must this be, since we're one in the body of Christ. There are also disagreements over family rights issues. In some conservative congregations, the definition of marriage has led to splits and break away denominations. These Christians must realize that they are all fighting for Christian values, although some are more traditional than others. Is it not true that we must not judge, for only God knows the content of our hearts? In these controversies, building bridges may not be as simple as it seems. Spiritually our road map is laden with impediments that continue to divide us. It's imperative that Christians make a greater effort to reach out in this murky landscape of doubt. It'll take the Holy Spirit to lead the way.

Thought of the Week

"The Spirit told me to go with them and not to make a distinction between them and us. These six brothers also accompanied me, and we entered the man's house."

—Act 11:12 (NRSV)

Meditation 7

Solidarity

In working together it's good to have a sense of solidarity. Be innovative and see the transforming power of the Holy Spirit at work in your midst. It'll be necessary to pay attention to your constituents and be an active coordinator of the workplace. By keeping your finger on the pulse of the group and knowing when an affirmation is in order, countless headaches will be staved off. In so doing, you'll be practicing good management skills while capturing the heart of the community. Through your example you'll be showing spiritual leadership.

Konrad von Gesner (1516–1565), a Swiss naturalist, photographer, and classical linguist noted, "Best of all is to preserve everything in a pure, still heart, and let there be for every pulse a thanksgiving, and for every breath a song." Von Gesner focuses on a holistic emphasis and thanksgiving for all things.

Put an Emphasis on Service

In your organization use your natural gift of leadership to rally others to fulfill the firm's objectives. Before doing so, it's wise to seek counsel from matured experts and experienced individuals in the office. English writer and clergyman Robert Burton (1577–1640) asked, "Who cannot give good counsel? 'tis cheap, it costs them nothing."

In some churches priests have even been known to wash the feet of women where such action was considered taboo. However, the goal of such demonstration of leadership is to motivate and enlist members to do the same. This is the spirit of humble service that's a true mission of sacredness.

Follow Willingly

To have a congregation follow, the hierarchical leadership has to be centered on respect of the followers of the ministerial hierarchy. The congregants must never think that they are being herded like cattle. It's best for them to volunteer for ministries within the church and have attendees see themselves as brothers and sisters in Christ. Such an attitude will invigorate the group. Members will be interacting with the spirit of goodwill and following through on the Word that's clear about their role in the church.

Rob McKenna (b. 1927), a Dominican bishop, now retired, known for his traditionalist Catholic positions—observed, "You can study government and politics in school, but the best way to really understand the process is to volunteer your time." McKenna's advice was not only meant for government and political enterprises but it's also appropriate in the church. For church members, this will mean volunteering in different committees, becoming familiar with their various programs, and becoming knowledgeable concerning how they work.

A Matter of Values
It's wise to want the best for all people. This means that everyone ought to be treated like a colleague who is vital to the organization. There must be awareness against the desire to be worldly. Everyone doesn't have to have a limousine to be considered successful in life. Good values and adequate behavioral norms are more important, for through these goals, to all our brothers and sisters, it'll be necessary to promote positive growth and competence beneficial to the organization. With spiritual excellence becoming a driving force within the group, its reach to the forsaken, by empowering and motivating them, will mean changes on the horizon.

Franklin D. Roosevelt (1882–1945), the thirty-second president of the United States assured us, "I'm not the smartest fellow in the world, but I can sure pick smart colleagues."

A leader, whether in government, politics or the church, must always have his or her eyes out for new talent. This untapped resource will give new vitality to a government, industry, or church. It's the basic foundation of a group's future. New talent strengthens growth and paves the way for the advancement of the best, for the benefit of the company. It's necessary that all hands play a role in this essential process, for it enhances a sense of solidarity that's always necessary for accomplishing an organization's goals.

Thought of the Week

"For whosoever exalteth himself shall be abased; and he that humbleth himself shall be exalted."

—Luke 14:11 (KJV)

Love Conquers

Meditation 8

Images of God

ALONG WITH THE Father and Son, the Holy Spirit is the third person of the Trinity. Christ was crucified and exalted and now sits on the right hand of the Father. Christ's birth was divinely inspired but He came into the world through his mother Mary. He was baptized by John the Baptist and pursued an earthly ministry. We Christians are part of the body of Christ, with Christ as the Head of the church. On the feast of Pentecost with the coming of the Holy Spirit the church began, and thousands became baptized Christians. Only God is spiritually perfect; he is our universal leader.

Mia Hamm (b. 1972), a retired soccer player remarked, "I am a member of a team, and I rely on the team, I defer to it and sacrifice for it, because the team, not the individual, is the ultimate champion." When she made such a statement Hamm must have been thinking about soccer, but much of it is true of the church of which we're all a part. It's all about fellowship, for with our social interactions we build each other up. We listen to fellow church members, we plan, organize, and we move forward as one body in Christ.

A Source of Life

Many Christians have come to know the power of God's anointing in their ministries. Only through his power do we rise to the qualifications of what it means to be godly. Jesus's character must be followed; this was demonstrated during his life and ministry. All things that characterize God's rule are those we must do. During Christ's earthly ministry he clearly demonstrated how faith and the spirit must work together. Believers in knowing the spirit of Christ will be led into deeper spiritual experiences. The only true way to become a spirit-filled evangelist is through the Lord. Such an evangelist is sure to tap into the outpouring of the Holy Spirit, and knows to speak the language of the Spirit.

This spirit is everywhere and in every place. We'll be edified by many Christians we meet who profess the Christian faith. Bill Gates (b. 1955), an American computer magnate and philanthropist observed, "Your most un-happy customers are your greatest source of learning." Even in unhappy cus-tomers and circumstances, the Christian spirit reveals himself as a discerning light he's alive and well.

False Inspiration

We'll know false inspiration when it's evil in character. Persons who dabble in such falsehoods work against the promises of God. These may well end up in grave spiritual danger. They lack a true apostolic spirit. The bad spirit has taken hold of them and doesn't build up the body of Christ. Evil spirits are known for their dissension, bitterness and falsehoods. Their teachings aren't in accordance with the Word of God. Albert Camus (1913–1960), a French Nobel Prize–winning author, journalist and philosopher felt, "The evil that is in the world always comes of ignorance, and good intentions may do as much harm as malevolence if they lack understanding."

Formal Professions of Faith

Faith calls for a commitment to Jesus Christ and, then be aglow in the spirit of God. Be certain as one of the many Christians that you've received the blessings of Abraham. As a child of God, you'll have a willing spirit of God that sustains all things. You'll come to know the timeless spiritual principles of your faithfulness and dedication to the Word of God. The fire of the

Holy Spirit will fill your life with all good things, and you'll be walking in the light.

It was Vince Lombardi (1913–1970), the head coach of the Green Bay Packers who realized, "The quality of a person's life is in direct proportion to their commitment to excellence, regardless of their chosen field of endeavor." Living a life for Christ and obeying his commandments are the epitome of a believer's excellence in living a successful life.

Thought of the Week
"For with God nothing shall be impossible."

—Luke 1:37 (KJV)

Meditation 9

Faces of Love
The faces of love are quite diverse and sustain all good things. Love unites people so they can live harmoniously and is the greatest creative force with which man is endowed. Loving calls for unblemished hearts that are pure and sincere. We sense this when the people that love and are in love display joyful hearts. Their hearts light up with joy that expresses much faithfulness. This is the foundation of authentic love. Early Christian theologian, philosopher and Bishop Saint Augustine (354–430 AD) described faith that is touched by love this way, " Faith is to believe what you do not see; the rewards of this faith is to see what you believe."

Evangelistic Love
Evangelistic love is one of friendship. It's the light that shines brightly for those we encounter. This flame fills our heart and touches souls. It must be this way because it's the expression of God's deep love for us. Christians who project this

type of love believe in heaven with all their hearts, for they have discovered the full meaning of truthful love of all things. Saints proselytize and become older as they grow in such a form of loving. In their encounter with the people a communion of love soon develops that becomes one that is centered on Christ. This is expressed through loving and helping the poor and needy in our midst. Such recipients of love will find themselves with new hearts as they encounter the living Christ. Older and matured saints have humble hearts and their actions are based on a leap of faith. Roman Catholic religious sister Mother Teresa (1910–1971) remarked, "Let us touch the dying, the poor, the lonely and the unwanted according to the graces we have received and let us not be ashamed or slow to do the humble work." She was teaching us that there ought to be no shame in serving the dying, unwanted, and poor living among us.

Communication of Love

Let us plan on loving the right way. Flowing within and from us will be love that reaches out to all. Such love is the greatest when it displays a real transformation in our family, neighbors, friends and those we encounter on the highways and byways of life, as we declare a heart full of peaceable love. It's this sort of caring that emanates from being with others we sincerely love. Such is the depth of love that we must hold up like a burning torch in our daily walk with Christ, while forming relationships and encouraging the rejected. Such communication is activated through the light of faith. Mahatma Gandhi (1869–1948) observed a negative aspect that might exist in such communication: "It has always been a mystery to me how men can feel themselves honored by the humiliation of their fellow beings." This form of communication may mislead and often be confusing to persons who wish to communicate in truth.

Love of Life

Oscar Wilde (1854–1900), an Irish author and playwright remarked, "Keep love in your heart. A life without it is like a sunless garden when the flowers are dead." Engrossment in self love that does not extend itself to others is not good. Such love is a disorderly sort. Love ought to be steadfast, promoting what is best in the world by touching those who feel unloved and isolated. We must love all our brothers and sisters by showing them that we really have their interests at heart. This is one of the basic concepts for creation. We know it when our hearts burn while reaching out to the elderly and young alike. Thus, there's no time to nurture hardened hearts that are filled with disillusion. Our goal must be to profess love from the warmth of our hearts. May our hearts be like those described by Morihei Ueshiba (1883–1969), a Japanese artist and founder of the martial art of aikido who believed, "Your heart is full of fertile seeds, waiting to sprout." Such sprouts will be an expression that seek all the good things in life by which we've been blessed.

These ingredients are the faces of love that are sending and touching many things in its path. Love's profundity can only be found in Jesus Christ, our Lord and Savior and through the working of the Holy Spirit.

Thought of the Week
"Charity suffereth long, and is kind; charity envieth not; charity vaunteth not itself, is not puffed up."

—1 Corinthians 13:4 (KJV)

Meditation 10

Beauty of Love
The beauty of love is all around us in this world, such as in nature, when we are graced by the golden rays of the sun amid the lush foliage in parks. During the summer months we view the crashing of the waves while strolling along the beach on a sunlit day. Or we observe the ice-covered mountains that grace the skyline in the distance.

In our daily walk with Christ, however, there are other true loves that are more personal and which we embrace on our journey through life. These consist of the people we love—our father, mother, aunts, uncles, cousins, relatives, neighbors and friends. Much of this love may be true, just and holy. We're attracted by a smile, laughter, attire, education, physical beauty, and or intellectual prowess. This abundant good in humankind reveals itself as the face of beautiful truth. It was Wayne Dyer (b. 1940), an American self-help author and motivational speaker who observed, "Doing what you love is the cornerstone of having abundance in your life." Much abundant beauty is all around for us to grasp.

In touching on abundance a basic principle is involved. American founding father and principal author of the Declaration of Independence Thomas Jefferson (1743–1826) realized, "Honesty is the first chapter in the book of wisdom." Indeed, in order to capture truth, beauty and wisdom, honesty is called for. Wise seers say we can embrace these gifts through perseverance during challenges in our attempt to do better and better each day. This process takes time and spiritual growth.

Faithful Love
To be truly in love calls for much dedication. Reaching out to this joy we come to a place where we'll embrace the Almighty One. His power is found in loving kindness that we show in our actions towards others. This is wondrous love at its best. It may seem evasive, but through consistency we'll be able to capture it. Faithful love is all around us. Imagine yourself undertaking a journey of sorts—life's journey of discovery. Profess a Catholic faith—that is the universal faith that has to do with all things. Become secure in your walk, by encountering a deep and lasting reality. An authentic undertaking brings joy to the soul. It's faithful love at its best. American cosmetic surgeon and author Maxwell Maltz (1889–1975) stated, "Man maintains his balance, poise, and sense of security only as he is moving forward." Faithful love is never stagnant. It's always on the move, embracing all things in its path.

Love of Christ
American screenwriter Monica Johnson (1946–2010) captured the essence of faith when she testified, "God is so unique in giving His people ways of

fellowship, witness, and remember what a mighty and merciful God He is." His love is through his Word. It reveals itself by loving the poor and the underdog. The Holy Spirit will deepen our love and reveal the greatest love of all. It's the love of the cross that's a symbol of our hope, resurrection, life, and salvation. Become an old saint who grows in love. It's the best value in life that brings true liberty and a pure heart. This is when you'll have a heart of flesh through the Spirit of Truth that comes from the Good Shepherd himself, embodying and witnessing His faith to us.

Love of Creation
Rabindranath Tagore (1861–1941), a Bengali author and artist of the late nineteenth century believed, "Love is the only reality and it is not mere sentiment. It is the ultimate truth that lies at the heart of creation." Tagore touches the pulse of love's characteristics. Most persons encounter love through the signs of God's love that are with us. Such liberty involves true beauty for it cleanses our hearts and souls. With such love new hearts are formed and nurtured, which leads to the charity of understanding different cultures, challenging us in our roles to be custodians of God's creation.

Community love will care for people in our villages, cities and towns. By so doing we'll follow the commandment to love our neighbor as ourselves. With such a commandment, we'll end up sowing love in all places by displaying the fruits of the Spirit. Love is a powerful source that creates and recreates, and as it does so, blesses everything in its path. This is one of the ultimate beauties of life that could best be described as boundless.

Thought of the Week
"Heal the sick, cleanse the lepers, raise the dead, cast out devils: freely ye have received, freely give."

—Matthew 10:8 (KJV)

Meditation 11

Cooperate In Love

When addressing people do you make distinctions between them? Do you see each person as special and different? Are you condescending to people? Do you pay attention to how they look, speak and are dressed? It appears that we all do these things in some form or the other. However, we ought to look beyond a person's physical exterior. Persons have to be treated with the utmost respect. This is a lesson we must always bear in mind when meeting people.

Are you into dazzling the world by what you do? Robert Browning (1812–1889) did this with poems, plays and pamphlets. His wife Elizabeth Barrett Browning (1806–1861) was more successful than her husband with her works. In Sonnet 43, she expressed a limitless love:

"With my lost saints—I love thee with the breath,
Smiles, tears, of all my life! - and, if God choose,
I shall but love thee better after death."

There was a superb distinction in this special love the Brownings shared. It was definitely a supreme love that knew no limits nor distinction. She would give her all for the love of saints.

Cooperate but Don't Control

Why would we try to control people when the best results come when we co-operate? This happens in the workplace, at play and in sports. American labor leader and civil rights activist Cesar Chavez (1927–1993) observed, "From the depth of need and despair, people can work together, can organize themselves to solve their own problems and fill their own needs with dignity and strength." In not seeing distinctions between management and workers—but with some cooperation—, any official can bring dignity to a work environment.

A Brazilian novelist and lyricist Paulo Coelho (b. 1947) noted, "I can control my destiny, but not fate. Destiny means there are opportunities to turn right or left, but fate is a one way street. I believe we all have the choice as to whether we fulfill our destiny, but our fate is sealed." Coelho cited the choices that we make for better or worse in our lives. He stressed the importance of making these, for these choices will determine the nature of the relationships we have. We must aim for relationships where there are no distinctions between a janitor and his or her boss. Everyone must be seen as working agreeably and jointly for the common good that benefits all.

Put Wings to Your Ideas

It takes love to put wings to ideas. How a person views the world is important. Such views will not be in your best interest like the novelist and poet Thomas Hardy (1840–1928), who saw the world governed by sheer chance and natural laws. Life is not a series of coincidences with bleakness, pessimism and irony. That's why by loving Christ Jesus, your life will be made whole. You will discover that a divine reality governs everything. This will be the sort of wings you must put to your ideas in dealing with others from every social strata. We all—regardless of class, distinctions and creed—must be loved, cared for and cherished.

Be Happy in Love

People must be happy and love one another. *Carpe Diem* is a Latin aphorism that means living to the fullest right now, for you have the opportunity "to seize the moment." A person's success is not merely, "Let us eat and drink, for tomorrow we die," as the Roman poet Horace (65–8 BC) stated; it's much more than that. It's being able to capture the true essence of living. It's imperative that we are active and caring members throughout our life's journey, loving others, and resisting distinctions between our families and friends. Jesus Christ urged us to love our neighbor as ourselves. Let your love be like that of the poet Christopher Marlowe (1564-1593) which he captured in "The Passionate Shepherd to His Love:"

"Come live with me, and be my love,
And we will all the pleasures prove

That valleys, groves, hills and fields,
Woods, or steepy mountain yields."

Or, like that of the poet and explorer Sir Walter Raleigh (1552(?)–1618) in "The Nymph's Reply to the Shepherd" - "To live with thee and be thy love."

Marlowe and Raleigh's love is engrossing and foremost on their minds. They would give anything for love, for it makes no distinctions. Jesus Christ's example was amazing when He died for us on the cross. His love was more than love between the sexes, fathers, mothers, brothers and sisters. It was a superior and special kind of love – boundless and distinctive for its saving grace.

Thought of the Week
"Take heed that ye do not your alms before men, to be seen of them: Otherwise ye have no reward of your Father which is in heaven."

—Matthew 6:1 (KJV)

Meditation 12

Acts of Love
Acts of love bring joy to precious hearts. In performing such acts, many look to the diversified fruits of love for God's grace. Through His grace this is done by a believer's life in showing God's love to all. Doing this calls for touching a love made in heaven that sustains precious souls and is brought about in Christ through the unification with the Holy Spirit of peace, prosperity and happiness. This is the good news that reaches out to every man, woman and child.

It takes a leap of faith to find security in Christ. Tullian Tchividjian (b. 1972), a professor of Theology and senior pastor of Coral Ridge Presbyterian

Church, Fort Lauderdale, Florida remarked, "Believe it or not, Christianity is not about good people getting better. If anything, it is good news for bad people coping with their failure to be good." What a demonstration it is, then, of an act of love to all those who have fallen short, while learning it takes redemption to succeed in a life of faith.

Sow Love

It's imperative that we love our neighbor. Show care and loving tenderness in every relationship. It's love that makes hope blossom like new petals after a rainstorm. Such is the revelation of the liberty of love that has to be nurtured. It's through trustworthy love that we will come to know beauty. Wondrous love is beyond comparison. It's the love sown that is found deeply intertwined in our hearts. Realization of this love can also be found in the symbolism of the cross. Some Christians wear it as a true display of Christ's promises that represent hope - life, death and the resurrection.

American author and aviator Anne Morrow Lindbergh (1906–2001) wrote, "For happiness one needs security, but joy can spring like a flower even from the cliffs of despair." How wonderful is God's security in a believer's life! It's the underpinnings of a assured love. Billy Graham (b. 1918), an American Christian evangelist thought, "God proved His love on the Cross. When Christ hung, and bled, it was God saying to the world, 'I love you.'"

Love and Serve

Put true love into practice. Let it be well-known and served to all individuals. To do so calls for a humble heart and a positive outlook. Love must be the love of his life. It ought to be authentic. Loving-kindness is vividly demonstrated during a Eucharistic celebration—the supper of the Lamb—, when the cross is lifted high for all to adore. Even the poor, needy and outcast are welcomed at this feast. This love is put into practice for all to ponder the goodness of Christ and his supreme love that is demonstrated for the common good.

It was Martin Luther King, Jr. (1929–1968), an American Baptist minister and leader of the African-American civil-rights movement who observed, "The ultimate tragedy is not the oppression and cruelty by bad people but the silence over that by the good people." Failure to sow love and make our voices heard could surely be the sort of tragedy within society to which King, Jr. alluded.

Be Recreated in Love

Desmond Tutu (b. 1931), a retired South African Anglican bishop stated, "You don't choose your family. They are God's gift to you, as you are to them." What a creation of love that Tutu touched on which is absolutely free to all. At a sublime level it's the love of connectedness. We contribute when we step forward to do our part in our community and the world at large. True love is created, recreated, and nurtured and it blossoms into amazing realities. It's just, holy and expresses the eternal goodness of the Creator.

Recreated love is a true gift to every living soul. Albert Camus (1913–1960), a French author, philosopher, and Nobel Prize winner captured this reality best when he noted, "Without culture, and the relative freedom it implies, society, even when perfect, is but a jungle. This is why any authentic creation is a gift to the future." We would hope that cycles of creative forces keep pushing us forward to tap into the dawning of a newer and better world. This could only be through the recognition and, acceptance of Jesus Christ, and the Holy Spirit that continue working miracles in our midst.

Thought of the Week

"If you love those who love you, what credit is that to you? For sinners love those who love them."

—Matthew 6:32 (NRSV)

Meditation 13

Discovering Love

Jodi Picoult (b. 1966), an American author who was awarded the New England Bookseller Award for fiction in 2003 observed, "You don't love someone because they're perfect, you love them in spite of the fact that they're not."

Some persons, especially young people, are rather confused about love. They ask, "What does it mean? Am I in love? How can I tell?" Many claim to be in love. Their passion may only be a mere attraction and based on overactive hormones. Some feel that they are sure that they are in love. "Love," they might claim, "hit me right between the eyes."

Others confuse love with sex. "If you love me, you'll go to bed with me." It's true that sex can be a healthy expression of love, but not always. Love is more subtle and has various meanings. It's deeper than you think. For example, Jesus Christ died for us on a cross. He gave his life so that we might have everlasting life. His act was the epitome of love. It's sacrificial love—agape is the greatest love of all.

Other Forms of Love

There are however other forms of love. Brotherly, sisterly and parental love are common. Scripture tells us that we must love our neighbor like ourselves. What you wish for yourself, wish for your neighbor. How you feel, feel the same way for others. What you do and enjoy, enjoy with him or her. There ought to be no difference between how you feel and think about yourself and of others.

Walk in Humility

We have to be humble in our walk of life and be sure to live in humility. Scripture reveals that we must even go a step further and love our neighbors greater that ourselves. What a duty that is. We'll all be negligent in doing so. Just imagine what such act will mean to us. Obviously, if we must love this way, we'll not be so puffed up about ourselves. We'll regard ourself as lesser than another individual. That will surely be a good thing, for our egos will not be so inflated.

We often hear people comparing themselves with others. Persons actually judge and boast about their accomplishments, declaring how great they are and how their coworkers don't have any experience compared with them. This is often a rather shameful display of pride. God is the provider of all our talents and gifts. We must give thanks to him for those we have. A person's talents and gifts can be here today and gone tomorrow. Nothing is promised to anyone. There's a season and time for everything under the sun.

Love in a Hospital

Imagine love when a spouse is in the hospital and his wife is beside him. He's in pain. His agony is great from the urinary tract infection that's systemic— the infection is in his blood stream. His wife is so concerned about him that she spends several nights at his side in his hospital room, even sleeping there with him. Throughout the day and night, nurses, doctors and care-givers come and go and the patient is unable to sleep. He's on tranquilizers to calm his nerves and watches the antibiotics anxiously from the saline drip. Being unable to move much, monitors keep him awake and he's in an agitated state. In the middle of the night while his wife sleeps on a nearby cot, he calls to her for help. She's exhausted from the stress and is trying to sleep, but he keeps waking her up. He wants a glass of water to comfort him. Next, he desires a blanket over his feet for he's cold. His wife hears his cries, each time crawling out of bed, and comforting him.

Of such is the essence of love. It's helping a broken-heart when it's in distress. His wife didn't have to be there. She could have been at home, but she cares deeply for her husband, and wants to help him. She'll do almost anything to comfort him. She always does so, by being with him through good and bad times. This is the sort of love Jesus Christ wants us to have and share with each other.

Thought of the Week

"...Give, and it will be given to you. A good measure, pressed down, shaken together, running over, will be put in your lap; for the measure you give will be the measure you get back."

—Luke 6:38 (NRSV)

Meditation 14

Pioneer of Salvation

Jesus Christ is the pioneer of our salvation. He's our savior from any danger, distress or bondage. Because of him, we've received blessings and joy, and we know that we're saved. In him, we're assured of living a resurrected life under his Lordship. Here we'll regain the glory through his grace. He's given us the power of the spirit willingly, because we're sons of the Most High. We've been emancipated and sanctified from evil that has befallen us. As a result, we'll glow in the promise of eternal life.

Tom Brokaw (b. 1940), an American TV journalist and the managing editor of NBC Nightly News from 1982 to 2004 remarked, "I think people of my generation became journalists—you know, right after the broadcast pioneer fathers—because we wanted to report the big stories." Brokaw was obviously explaining how a pioneer influenced some journalists' decision in pursuing a career in news. Nevertheless, the biggest story for Christians was about the pioneer of salvation, our Lord and Savior, Jesus Christ, of whom we're followers and adherents.

Pressures of the World

Because of what Christ accomplished on the cross at Calvary, his work has become a bastion against disease, suffering and death. No longer do we have to fear disease, because Christ is the greatest healer and there's a true purpose in all things under the sun. He's our fort against natural and unnatural disasters and destructive forces. However, we've witnessed God's divine wrath on unbelievers, who are many that live in ignorance of the truth about eternal life. Some of those have been haunted by demons, the fear of hell, meaningless lives, abuses, ignorance, and a total lack of understanding. But Christ understands our dilemma, and are always willing to forgive and save us from these afflictions.

Helen Thomas (1920–2013), an American author and a member of the White House press corps observed, "We don't go into journalism to be popular. It is our job to seek the truth and put constant pressure on our leaders until we get answers." If it's all about finding answers, we must turn to Jesus Christ as the most reliable source. In every matter, he's the epitome of truth. For a journalist and non-journalist, the Holy Spirit will enable us to explore new and untapped dimensions of the truth.

Bondage of Futility

Around the world, many people are living defeated lives. They are subject to oppression, social decay and want for many of the basic necessities of life. People have turned to political leaders for deliverance, but are often disappointed. In the news we witness much guilt and disappointment when it comes to solving economic and social issues. Some people throw their hands up in despair, for they can't believe the bad habits displayed by some of these politicians, in whom they have put their trust to make conditions better. There's alienation of the races when it comes to finding solutions for race relations. Voters are at each other throats and find themselves caught up in narrow ideological perspectives. That's why many tend to give up about finding solutions in this world. But, the Prince of Peace is alive and well, and he's eager to intervene, if we'll only let him.

Nelson Mandela (1918–2013), a South African anti-apartheid revolutionary and politician, who served as president of South Africa from 1994 to 1999 stated, "We pledge ourselves to liberate all our people from the continuing bondage of poverty, deprivation, suffering, gender and other discrimination."

These words from Mandela, praiseworthy as they may sound, desire the commitment of those that are in allegiance with Christ. It must be remembered that there's much that we don't understand about people's motives. Many live in bondage because of all sorts of ills, but it'll take faith and a belief in God to really set them free. Much admired work has been done on many continents by missionaries and many others, who are known to live and govern in godly ways.

It was Abraham Lincoln (1809–1865), the sixteenth president of the United States who believed, "Nearly all men can stand adversity, but if you want to test a man's character, give him power." Jesus who was "fully man and God" (Hebrews 2:5-18 NRSV) has passed this test. It's for us to emulate him and follow the only pioneer of salvation for all eternity. He's the most glorious and outstanding model who deserves all love, praise and glory.

Thought of the Week

"What then are we to say about these things? If God is for us, who is against us?"

—Romans 8:31 (NRSV)

Light Is a Force

Meditation 15

Our Light of Life

OUR LIGHT OF life can be made to burn brightly. It's the light that is already within us, one of faith that enlightens our humble minds. It's ideal that we radiate such light. By doing so, we dispel all darkness that is bent on engulfing us. Such light is a free gift—one of the greatest gifts. It's supernatural and has been a part of us from creation. It's a gift of faith and piety. Dutch Renaissance humanist, Catholic priest and theologian Desiderius Erasmus (1466–1536) said, "Give light, and the darkness will disappear of itself." This is why light in our life is a powerful source which reveals the truth.

O Light Eternal

Christians are the light of the world. They demonstrate this by their walk, talk and demeanor. Some persons in common parlance refer to them as angels of life among us. They are the light that brightens darkness and mirrors the stars that twinkle in the sky on a moonlit night. Through them many have come to discover peace—a peace in their hearts and joy in their hearts and minds. With their focused beams there will be the light of love shining brightly, revealing the truth of love. This is when beauty is captured in all its glorious hopefulness. It was Wendell Berry (b. 1934), an American novelist, poet and environmental activist who remarked, "To cherish what remains of the Earth and to foster its renewal is our legitimate hope of survival." Our light is the earth's hope.

Light of Peace
Imagine a flicker of light that transforms a scene from darkness revealing its true essence. With true light comes instruments of peace. It's best when such peace begins in an American home and spreads out throughout the many homes, villages and societies in the world. That demonstrates how when peace is planted it grows until it bears much fruit. We know how it feels without peace—when there's constant torment that irks our souls. So it's ideal to play our part in pursuing peace even with our next door neighbor, remembering that much good can be accomplished through your friendships.

There are steps in achieving this dream of peace. We do so by persevering and by working out a neighborly and peaceful existence. Once accomplished we have touched the gift of peace. This is done through light and courage. An American professional surfer Bethany Hamilton (b. 1990) was convinced that, "it's easy to look at the things of this world to solve our challenges and obstacles to life, but when we submit our lives to Christ, His grace, mercy, peace and love will bring through fulfillment to our lives." Real peace can only come to our lives through resolutions that involve the working of the Holy Spirit.

Light of the Gospel
A Chinese politician and philosopher Confucius (551–479 BC) revealed, "Life is really simple, but we insist on making it complicated." This is so true! It's easy to read the Gospels and grasp what has to be done to live in the light. By such scripture readers will be strengthened, enlightened and brought to life. Darkness will be banished from their thoughts and actions. They will cultivate the type of a character that renews their life while being transformed into a new being of light.

Jesus Christ, the Prince of Peace will be their ideal. They will walk with Christ and talk with him. Their conscience will become a flame of hope. The Prince of Peace will be their teacher, guardian, and provider.

Much of what they do will be revealed in a new life and the city where they live will be transformed to a city of peace. This is when the true message of the Gospels goes out to all capturing souls, filling them with peace and serenity. Martin Luther King Jr. (1929–1968) thought, "Life's most persistent and urgent question is, 'What are you doing for others?'"

With our lights we have to heal the brokenhearted. Go into the highways and byways and greet the poor and disenfranchised telling them that a new day has dawned. There we'll gather up the homeless and guide the poor and needy into paths of righteousness. With these actions, we'll be pushing the light of peace, love and truth into every nook and cranny of our daily walk.

Thought of the Week
"In the same way, let your light shine before others, so that they may see your good works and give glory to your Father in heaven."

—Matthew 5:16 (NRSV)

Meditation 16

Radiate Your Light
By the way you live let your light radiate to all men. Your speech and actions must tell your story. There must be brightness in your character that casts out the darkness of doubt. Shine like the sun, twinkle like a star and be at peace in the world. Share your love, spread it around to everyone—the happy and unhappy, rich, poor, hungry and homeless. Share uplifting thoughts, spread your wisdom as you meet friends, strangers and the unforgotten. An American author Wilferd Peterson (1900–1995) wrote, "Let your light shine. Be a source of strength and courage. Share your wisdom. Radiate love."

Another American poet and writer Wheeler Wilcox (1850–1919) observed, "The man who radiates good cheer, who makes life happier wherever he meets it, is always a man of vision and faith." Can we forgive and forget indiscretions? Must we forgive hurt when it's done, and those who suffer abuse experience pain? What about those individuals who make life a living hell? Can we forget the wrongs of those that are rude, cruel and offensive? Despite the nature of these wrongs, we must still forgive our friends, neighbors, strangers and enemies. Notice what social critic and former professor of psychiatry of the State University of New York Thomas Szasz (1920–2012) stated, "The stupid neither forgive nor forget, the naïve forgive and forget, the wise forgive but do not forget." To be wise in forgiving, forgiveness must be handled with finesse.

Be Polite in Thoughts and Actions

As the saying goes, "Always kill with kindness." It's good and sensible to acknowledge acts of kindness. Send thank-you cards, notes of appreciation, and give peace offerings to those with whom you don't see eye to eye. By doing what is right and just, you'll be expressing generosity by taking the high road. Do favors, especially to the least among us. Encourage friends, pat them on their backs, say a few nice words to those who are down and out, and encourage them. Never give up such an attitude. When conflicts arise, think of what you'll say and do. An unknown writer wrote, "We greatly influence others with our thoughts, if our thoughts are kind, peaceful and quiet, turned only toward good, then we also influence ourselves and radiate peace all around us." We must therefore watch our thoughts impact others and situations for the better.

Bend over backward, do a favor, and give and build confidence in people. It's a time to compliment, support and acknowledge the good things people do. This is what Mother Teresa of Calcutta (1910–1997) did. It was she who taught, "Let no one come to you without leaving better and happier. Be the living expression of God's kindness. Kindness in your face, kindness in your eyes, kindness in your smile." Mother Teresa's expressions are surely God-inspired kindness.

A Christian Demeanor in Society
Like Jesus, Christians must be a light unto the world. Modeling Christ, they must be living symbols of the good news to mankind. Their light must not be hidden nor dimmed, but must always shine brightly on those they meet. Why hide your light under a bushel? Christians' work is for all to see. It's hoped that through their life, persons will come to know the Lord and glorify him. In everything they must give thanks. As they reach out to people they must do so joyfully. In wonderful ways, these believers must touch the repentant and un-repentant alike.

Christians by their demeanor and calling will be able to make the Word known to those they encounter. By ministering, if believers are able to reach one lost sheep, they must consider that this was what they were called to do. They have to be wise according to their status in life. The hallmark of their faith will be simplicity and humility. When meeting people, it must be a positive experience, for their walk is crowned with a light that is truly brilliant.

Thought of the Week
"You are the light of the world. A city built on a hill cannot be hid."

—Matthew 5:14 (NRSV)

Meditation 17

Who Are You?
Who are you? If you were to be asked such a question you will probably answer it in an obvious way, such as, "My name is Clinton Harris. I'm thirty years old. As you can see I'm a self-employed African American male who

repairs computers in Lincoln City, Oregon. I'm Catholic and love the Portland Trailblazers." That's fine. However, there can be much more to your answer.

"Who Am I?" is a Christian song by Casting Crowns. It's more of a prayer for confused and lost souls. "Who Am I?" (1998) is also the title of a movie by directors Benny and Jackie Chan, in the Internet movie database that tells about a secret agent who lost his memory. He didn't know who he was. "Who am I?" has been the title of a quest in games, riddles, and quizzes, while a Christian may ask, "Who am I in Christ?"

Individuals who are serious about answering this question have turned to the Internet to look at Dr. Ann Dranistaris's questionnaire. In doing so, they will be able to find some answers to the following questions:

- Am I nurturing, caring and supportive?
- Am I loyal and supportive?
- Am I rigid and over-controlling?
- Am I responsible and spontaneous?
- Am I knowledgeable and creative?
- Am I secure and altruistic?
- Am I a stabilizer like the rock of Gibraltar?

Who Am I?" Is Important

Knowing the answer to "who am I in Christ?" tops the list of searches on the Internet. It's so for many reasons, because you'll be looking to the head of all principalities and powers, who has freed you from sin and death. Through him, you can pray for healing and, the ability to lay hands on the sick, and then be led victoriously through the storms of life. Your overall ability to do all things will be fostered and you'll be known for your good works.

To be a co-heir with Christ is an astounding blessing. As his divine ambassador, many will be touched by your presence and be willing to emulate a Christian lifestyle. You, in being part of a royal priesthood will shine your light brightly in a broken world. You'll be filled with mercy, kindness, humility, and long-suffering. Having been redeemed from the curse of sin, sickness and poverty, you'll be living victoriously in praising and thanking God. The devil and his schemes will flee from you because you'll be able to resist him in the name of Jesus. God has not given us a spirit of fear, but the power of love and a sound mind, for the Holy Spirit dwells with us.

Pick Up Your Cross

Join forces with other believing Christians and raise your cross high. You're a new creation in Christ and are on the front lines of the battle. Your salvation is assured as your role is to win souls for the Lord. This is done through your interaction with ordinary people who you meet on the highways and byways of life. It's for you to comfort and guide them to know God's blessings and promises. These souls must be consoled and reminded—and if they haven't done so, they should accept Christ, read the the Gospels of Hope, and at all times put their faith in the Lord. That's your responsibility and who you are in Christ.

Thought of the Week

"Yet if any of you suffers as a Christian, do not consider it a disgrace, but glorify God because you bear this name."

—1 Peter 4:16 (NRSV)

Meditation 18

Cherished Lives

Christians enjoy cherished lives. They are sure that their walk is blessed and guided by the loving Creator. Often, many congregate in fellowship with other believers. There, they find a deep joy in Gospel readings. The oil of gladness is reflected on their faces because they were anointed by the Holy Spirit. Their commitment to doing good works is crowned with their excellent service to mankind.

Robert Pirsig (b. 1928), an American writer stated, "When people are fanatically dedicated to political or religious faiths or any kind of dogmas or goals, it's always because these dogmas or goals are in doubt." A true Christian's belief is never fanatical. It's based on the sound biblical teachings of our Lord and Savior, Jesus Christ. Model Christians are not members of cults and don't embrace their calling solely through whim or by the urgings of a charismatic figure. Christians are sober, humble and meek at heart.

A Proud Christian

Christians are blessed with contrite hearts. Their love is profound and reaches out to all they meet. For them, love knows no discrimination for it's balanced and fair-minded. We see this when they do volunteer work with and for charities. Christians are strong and courageous. Their foundation is built on rock, so when the storms of life come, they are able to withstand the onslaught of mighty winds. In manifesting and cultivating care and tenderness of souls, they will be true models in their community. Through mere strength and calmness, they know what it is to dance with Mary, Mother of Joy. Within and from them, great streams of happiness flow to everyone. Even in times of trial and tribulation, they are remarkable barometers of stability, goodness and peace.

Christians are like good seed planted in fertile soil. Matthew 13:22 (NRVS) was clear: "As for what was sown among thorns, this is the one who hears the word, but the cares of the world and the lure of wealth choke the word, and it yields nothing." Good believers are never unfruitful. They keep growing and bearing abundant fruit - for they know that their Heavenly Gardener will keep pruning their dead branches, to ensure that there will always be an abundant harvest.

Christians of the Light

Like Christ, Christians are blessed with merciful hearts, and their patience is modeled after him. They display remarkable understanding and are slow to anger. Their care and protecting spirit are infectious. As a bride of Christ's church, they find great comfort in evangelizing. This ministry is one filled with constant joy, for even when they suffer setbacks, they know that Christ is present and will strengthen them. William Shakespeare (1564–1616), a greatly renowned English playwright and poet expressed it best with Iago to Roderigo in *Othello*:

"How poor are they that ha' not patience! What wound did ever heal but by degrees?"

Christians must always be patient. It's the prize of the race that counts. At times the going may be slow and difficult, but they must persevere. Never doubt, for through God's grace there will be unforeseen miracles on the horizon.

Christian Witnessing

Margaret Mitchell (1900–1949), an American author and journalist with the *Atlanta Constitution*, reported Scarlett O'Hara in *Gone with the Wind* (1936), as saying, "I'm going to live through this, and when it's over, I'm never going to be hungry again. No, nor any of my folks. If I have to steal or kill—as God is my witness, I'm never going to be hungry again."

Unlike Mitchell's depiction of witnessing, a Christian's approach is guided spiritually and in the process he doesn't sin or threaten. Many Christians witness by a demeanor of sacredness. With the Holy Spirit, he's a symbol of joy and tells freely about Christ's resurrection and his promises for mankind. His effusive kindness adapts and changes to every situation but his message is the same—give your life to Christ, for he died for you on the cross at Calvary. He was resurrected, ascended into heaven, and now sits at the right hand of God the Father. Still, a Christian's testimony is new every morning, for the scripture by which he or she lives is spirit and life. This is always his revelation, for he's blessed by knowing the truth about eternal life.

Thought of the Week

"He that loveth his life shall lose it; and he that hateth his life in this world shall keep it unto life eternal."

—John 12:25 (KJV)

Precious Gifts

Our Marvelous Gifts

C HRISTIANS DISCOVER THEIR gifts as they travel down the road of life. One such gift is witnessing and helping others in a way that results in a call to be gracious in love. But the purpose of this gift is not only to enrich people—the poor and well-to-do alike—, but to be a shining light in their midst. To accomplish these blessings it's necessary to engage in an active spiritual lifestyle. French Enlightenment writer, historian and philosopher Voltaire (1694–1778) wrote, "God gave us the gift of life; it is up to us to give ourselves the gift of living well." It is just to focus on four superb gifts of life—nature, knowledge, peace and the Holy Spirit.

Gift of Nature

A liberal politician, philanthropist and scientist John Lubbock (1834–1913) observed, "Earth and sky, woods and fields, lakes and rivers, the mountains and the sea, are excellent schoolmasters, and teach some of us more than we can ever learn from books." With an ecologically consciousness mind, there's much talk and some action about caring for nature by being stewards in protecting God's creation. Everyday we must care for the earth's immensity of trees, lakes, rivers, streams, mountains and valleys and experience the surge of new life of birds, fishes and an abundance of wildlife in our parks, forests and jungles. Unlike the information in books, Lubbock felt that nature teaches many things, while providing joy, comfort, food, clothing and medicine.

Gift of Knowledge

Classical Greek philosopher Socrates (470/469–399 BC) proposed, "To know, is to know that you know nothing. That is the meaning of true knowledge." Here, Socrates seems to focus on our senses, which are often deceptive in a constantly changing world. At times, even in science when empirical studies are conducted, there are still observational errors. Some experience the throes of life through hardships, difficulties and illnesses that may teach lessons. As we try deciphering life's many questions, our thought-processes remain polluted by our undeveloped senses. Over years of devoted study, we're still left wondering what has happened to the knowledge that we once thought was true and accurate? With changes in living we might conclude like the preeminent English poet, playwright and actor William Shakespeare (1564–1616), that "ignorance is the curse of God; knowledge the wing wherewith we fly to heaven." Knowledge depends on finding the truth that can only be discovered through the Holy Spirit.

Gift of Peace

Indian politician Mahatma Gandhi (1869–1948) remarked, "An eye for an eye only ends up making the whole world blind." That's why forgiving others for wrongs done is important. By tasting life's possibilities and becoming open channels of peace, we must continue to touch lives. It'll be good to practice pure living and view it as one's mission to perpetuate such living. It must be a lifestyle that a believer sustains by being a witness concerning the good lessons learned about life. This is why a constant dialogue with a conflicting party is essential. As the German born physicist Albert Einstein (1879–1955) noted, "Peace cannot be kept by force; it can only be achieved by understanding." In order to find common ground, problems that arise between leaders, societies and nations have to be confronted and discussed.

Gift of the Holy Spirit

The Holy Spirit is a free gift from God. He's the greatest gift that a believer can have. Undoubtedly, he's a life-giving force who is the light of life. Through his spirit a Christian will enjoy a supreme quality of life—one that is illuminated, new and filled with the experience of everlasting love. Such an indwelling of the spirit is sustained by a lifestyle of caring and compassion toward others. This is done through walking in simplicity and humility. By living a pious life, a believer will share in the everlasting and abiding truth of the spirit. It's the senior pastor of the First Baptist Church of Atlanta, Georgia, Charles Stanley (b. 1932), who testified, "Earthly wisdom is doing what comes naturally. Godly wisdom is doing what the Holy Spirit compels us to do."

Thought of the Week

"Every good gift and every perfect gift is from above, and cometh down from the Father of lights, with whom is no variableness, neither shadow of turning."

—James 1:17 (KJV)

Meditation 20

Our Daily Bread

God intended that our daily bread sustains us. As we're nurtured and are being filled in the process we find much joy. Feasting on the fruits of the earth is an amazing gift. These come after toil, but the soil has to be prepared in the right way to bear such fruits. It's often thrilling to see an abundance of produce that's used for the common good. This is such an exceptional blessing. It's written in the Bible that our bread is more than a meal, and it includes every word that proceeds out of the mouth of God. Indian spiritual master Sai Baba (1838–1918) taught, "Life is a song—sing it. Life is a game—play it. Life is a challenge—meet it. Life is a dream—realize it. Life is a sacrifice—offer it. Life is love—enjoy it." This description amply describes the nature, and scope of our bread of life.

Pureness of Living

French sculptor and graphic artist Camille Claude (1864–1943) explained, "I am in no mood to be deceived any longer by the crafty devil and false character whose greatest pleasure is to take advantage of everyone." Why don't we then become lights of life? This spiritual undertaking will sustain our hearts with love. By so doing we'll be heading down the road with faithful souls who are traversing the earth. These individuals have peace and live joyful lives in the hope and security of Christ. These saints are blessed souls not ensnared by the pleasure of spoiled and tainted spiritual food. Superfluous things do not faze them for they keep on moving to glory, and walking in the spirit as messengers and witnesses to our world.

Keep Moving Forward

Being fed with the right sort of bread, Christians keep moving forward in this broken world. In their daily walk, they often times behold our heart's beauty. We can hear shouts of joy and see their delight when they feed a fallen soul. We can spot them visiting the lonely who are locked away in nursing and convalescent homes. Through their ministry, they help the weak and feeble of heart by bringing love to their lives. They aren't concerned if some view their efforts as failures. To them, they are doing God's work—laboring in the fields for the welfare of souls, watering the earth, planting seeds and awaiting the harvest. With their efforts, inseparable bonds are formed and nurtured with the disenchanted. In the right places and with the right people—as architects of change in Christ, they will form deep and lasting friendships with the disenchanted.

Making Smart Choices

By embracing all peoples, we must face the music and become shields and protectors of God's creation, which is to be fed and beautified. It was Mahatma Gandhi (1869–1948), a leader of India's independence movement, who observed, "The greatness of a nation and its moral progress can be judged by the way its animals are treated. I hold that the more helpless a creature the more entitled it is to protection by man from the cruelty of humankind."

Having bread does mean that we must climb every mountain to make life livable for all God's creatures. For when you think about it, animals sustain us with food, clothing, medicine, protection, comfort, and pleasure. We must not be tempted by alluring desires to exploit their gifts, and not build and rekindle them in the right way for future generations. In faithfulness, our dreams call for trusting our God-given instincts in living the best possible lives we can. We must thank God for his blessings for the bounty that he has graciously provided for us.

For all that we have been blessed with, we must continually pray and sing hymns of praise, and thanksgiving to God. It's God in his infinite wisdom that has provided us with an abundance of breads. We must always remember to glorify him for his wonderful acts. It's clear that through nature's diversification, he has given us many choices that we can only imagine what faith and trust he has in us—the joy of his creation. This joy climaxes at the pinnacle of his feast of feasts—the Eucharist—which takes place every Sunday, and most weekdays in churches, or during home liturgies.

Thought of the Week
"Jesus answered him, It is written, 'One does not live by bread alone.'"

—Luke 4:4 (NRSV)

Meditation 21

Blessing in Disguise
What does it mean to have glorious opportunities? Yes, you did attend one of the best universities in the United States, and there you received an outstanding education. Having landed a top job at a prestigious law firm, you're moving up in your career. What else did you achieve? You married the man or woman of your dreams and are a parent of three wonderful children. You

like taking chances, so you bought a raffle ticket and hit the jackpot. What else has enhanced your life of dreams? You have become a well-known motivational speaker with numerous engagements. Having met life's challenges with success, you conclude that you have been blessed with God-given opportunities.

Turned Upside Down

Sometimes a misfortune has a strange way of changing a life. You didn't expect to be diagnosed with dementia. You have become like the British retired medical professional, Dr. Jennifer Bute who was diagnosed with this same disease. In "Dementia: A Glorious Opportunity" by Kreativity on Vimeo on April 26, 2011, Dr. Bute told the public of her remarkable years as a general practitioner, and all the wonderful things she did for her patients. Talking about her disability, though - not with discontentment, she now views her affliction as a glorious opportunity from God to do a lot more good for people. Will the average Joe be like Dr. Bute?

Joe's dreams, plans and fortunes have been thrown into disorder, and everything seems to be in disarray. His whole life's landscape has been rearranged and transformed. What sort of dilemma has his situation become? His life has been turned upside down and everything seems as though it has been changed for the worse. Some of his friends appear to misunderstand his misfortune, but to what extent is his affliction a misfortune? Other loving friends and neighbors rally around him for being such a superb role model in his church and community.

6cyclemind, a Filipino band that plays alternative music, sings about Joe's phenomenon in having his world turned "Upside Down." The band released two albums—*Shine* (2003) and *Panorama* (2005). Presently, his situation can be likened to a person that now has to do metaphorical handstands, headstands and somersaults to get through life, for he's contemplating life-changes like those of Dr. Bute, to cope with the new person he has become.

Missed Your Chance?

Some may feel as if Joe has missed the chance of a lifetime. You may experience emptiness while afflicted with a debilitating disease. But isn't it right to say that when one door closes another opens? American philosopher and poet Ralph Waldo Emerson (1803–1882) observed, "For everything you have missed, you have gained something else, and for everything you gain, you lose something else." Viewing your situation as gain and not as loss will put untold benefits in your life. Why not be like Dr. Bute?

View your life as having a new quality and meaning, while imagining new ways of thinking and coping. It's like starting over one's life from scratch but be assured that everything will work out for the best. Strange as it may seem, dementia like that experienced by Dr. Bute and Joe, can be a blessing in disguise. A person must realize that he or she is bearing this cross for the long haul. It's good for him or her to reflect on the newness of his or her nature, for God sees us all as complete—the afflicted and unafflicted alike. Sufferers will have to consider themselves as being, valuable members of society, for in life we have to be calm and confident in the face of trials and tribulations.

Quality Of Life

Promoting your general well being when living with dementia is important. It's necessary to become more physical, let a friend accompany you for walks, and live in a life-affirming community. Challenge yourself in new ways. Monitor your ability to read and if you can't, find someone who will read to you. Be certain to gear all activities toward the growth and development of your emotional, physical and mental health. As the disease progresses be sure that your finances and social aspects of your life are in order. American author, salesman, and motivational speaker Zig Ziglar (1926–2012) pointed out, "Fact: If standard of living is your number one objective, quality of life almost never improves. But if quality of life is your number one objective, standard of living invariably improves." Being a person with dementia, your life like other suffering patients will improve because your focus and priority will be based on having quality treatment.

Thought of the Week

"(Yet the Lord your God refused to heed Balaam, the Lord your God turned the curse into a blessing for you, because the Lord your God loved you.)"

—Deuteronomy 23:5 (NRSV)

Meditation 22

A Good Person

Being a good person can mean different things to different people. Some may consider helping others as the most important characteristic. It doesn't matter what nature of help it is. It could mean bringing a friend a meal when he or she is sick, or giving a glass of water to a thirsty beggar. A person's reason for doing such an act is important. Are you doing such service to be praised? Are you going to pat yourself on your back saying how wonderful you are?

There are people who consider themselves good because they give willingly to charitable causes like the Salvation Army, cancer society, mental health, diabetes, Alzheimer's, or cystic fibrosis. Some though may participate in walks for finding cures and raising money to benefit charitable organizations. Such persons are also thought of as being good by many.

Having a Trustworthy Character

It's one thing to be helpful but another to be trustworthy. Are you reliable? Do you go that extra mile to help someone? Some persons devote themselves completely to a cause or causes and give their all. Do you feed the poor? How often do you distribute food at your local food bank? Or, do you do volunteer work at church, hospital or the library?

We'll agree that these are some things that good people do. But are you honest? Do you cheat on your income taxes? It is known that a few will inflate their numbers when it comes to charitable donations. It may be that some

— 53 —

people allow things to slip and do not keep adequate records of their gifts. Persons are known also, to fudge on their medical expenses. How do you regard yourself? Are you still as good and dependable as you think you are? Are you like a rock to others, or merely shifting sand?

Goodness and Holiness

It's well known that we're all sinners. Some of the greatest saints were known to have tarnished backgrounds. For example, St. Augustine (354–430 AD), one of the fathers of the Catholic Church, lived a rather rambunctious life in his youth. For years, he was a wild man, although he was a learned intellectual. In his moving book, *Confessions*—the first spiritual autobiography ever written—he extrapolated on his troubling deeds that he greatly regretted. Yet, he was saved by God, and much of today's theology of the Catholic Church was shaped by him.

A saint who died at the age of twenty-four and who was of exceptional holiness is eighteenth-century's St. Thérèse of Lisieux. She prayed for suffering for redemptive purposes, wrote the *Story of a Soul,* and as a Carmelite nun, she was steadfast in her faith. St. Thérèse because of her dedication to what she described as "the small way" viewed us to be like "little children," for she thought that this was how we must be to enter the kingdom of God. As the second female doctor of the universal church, she foresaw that through goodness, there would grow the faithfulness of innocence.

Well-Liked People

To be a good person is not always a matter of how well-liked a person is, but how genuine the heart in the eyes of God. This is simply a state of being good, benevolent and committed to the Christian faith.

We must always be willing to accept God's will for us. At its best, this means being pious and virtuous. For when we accept Jesus Christ, it's a belief in Agathism—that all things incline toward good. We will be Agathists, when our actions are well-intentioned, and lead to immense personal and social reforms.

Thought of the Week

"...So that you may be children of your Father in heaven; for he makes his sun rise on the evil and on the good, and sends rain on the righteous and on the unrighteous."

—Matthew 5:45 (NRSV)

Meditation 23

To Be Truly Rich

Are you rich in the things of this world? Are these riches satisfying to your soul? If the answer is no, look at what it means to have the right kind of riches.

There are people in this world who have more than enough material possessions. They boast about their money, property, and wealth. They go on extravagant vacations and, stay at luxurious hotels, but they are not satisfied. Some possess fine paintings and sculptures— which are expensive, elaborate, and elegant—by renowned artists, and will often display them for public viewing. Yet these masterpieces don't bring them satisfaction.

Some wealthy persons are owners of elaborate yachts, live in luxurious mansions, drive state-of-the-art cars, and have many admirers, but they are still dissatisfied with their possessions. What if their friends are of a good nature and have fine qualities—sweet and affable—but still their lives don't seem right to them?

While drinking the finest wines and champagne, these folks attend the best concerts, enjoy classical music, and cheer sopranos with melodious voices. Being dressed in stunning evening attire and flowing gowns, still something is missing. Their fragrance is that of expensive perfumes and colognes, and driven by chauffeurs they grace elaborate parties, but they still may feel out of place.

These individuals may enjoy some of the best things that the world has to offer. Their friends are elegant, have a quick wit, and sense of humor, but what isn't amusing is that they may come away from events feeling that life is meaningless, and they still have to find themselves. They may ask themselves, "Who am I? What am I doing? What am I trying to prove? Where must I go from here? What's my future?"

Searching for an Answer
It could be that they may have to downsize and start enjoying the many simple things of life they have been overlooking all along, cutting out the extravagance. A more realistic step will be to give their lives to Jesus Christ—pick up their cross and follow him who watches over every aspect of our lives and who knows our hearts. It may not be easy being rich, but ironically there is much more to be gained when Christians live modestly. This shift comes after those who are rich reach a point of determining what will endure forever, and what's most important in life.

Such people must have an eye on the prize for things eternal. It's believed by the faithful that if you have Christ, you have everything that is and will be necessary for your journey. Can wealth buy health, satisfaction, happiness, joy and peace of mind? Over and over again, we read scriptures that warn us about being rich in the world, We have to be careful about our earthly possessions for they may own us by becoming our gods. Instead, put your hope in God's heavenly kingdom and God's gifts, which is where our real future lies.

The Gift of True Happiness
True happiness brings peace of mind. How do we have peace of mind? By serving the Lord and Savior, Jesus Christ and being a light to others. It's true that we have to enjoy the basic necessities and have enough money to live—food, clothing and shelter—but these blessings we must share with the poor and destitute. Living just for oneself is dangerous. Many famous people have regretted not living godly lives. Do not become one of them.

An English archbishop during the reign of Henry VIII bemoaned the fact that if he had served God as faithfully as he had served his king, he would have forgiven him in his old age. During the sixteenth century, Cardinal Wolsey who was stricken with a broken heart, was executed by King Henry VIII.

Thought of the Week

"For you know the generous act of our Lord Jesus Christ, that though he was rich, yet for your sakes he became poor, so that by his poverty you might become rich."

—2 Corinthians 8:9 (NRSV)

Meditation 24

Finding the Authentic You

What are you letting into your life? Are you living true to yourself? Have you considered your life's mission? Do you have goals to create a new vision for yourself? Well, it's a time to engage in perpetual seeking. What are your intentions? Are you open to infinite possibilities? If you are not considering taking action on these questions, you will rob yourself of the chance to discover the real you. By undertaking your discovery, you'll not only expand your mind but also build up resilience. Your outlook about life will improve and you'll begin seeing a world of possibilities.

Practice and Exercise

Your goal is to achieve a balanced self. This calls for listening to your body, breathing in fresh air, taking long walks, listening to music, and meditating. These opportunities will provide ways for you to enjoy the sunshine, dream, and practice self-healing. These are all means of caring for yourself. Inevitably you'll need to engage in honest conversations with your loved ones. Do this at a time when you don't have to answer the phone nor send emails. Use your breaks for physical workouts and hobbies.

Put time aside for other vital purposes, like seeking knowledge and developing your mind. Joseph Addison (1672–1719), an English playwright and politician observed, "Reading is to the mind what exercise is to the body." Your object must be to build both body and mind. But first, ask yourself what's right with you. Some persons approach life wrongly by focusing on negative attributes that jump out at them. You must have been doing some things right in your life that you may not be taking credit for.

Moral Stamina
It's time to be responsible for your actions. Find peace in the world by practicing peacemaking with your neighbors and friends. Ask yourself the hard questions and explore ways of making decisions better. Do not succumb to quick fixes or delight in the world's mediocrity. In all things, quality must be your goal. In doing these things, you'll then be launching yourself on a journey of self-improvement. Having an open mind, you'll discover that issues are not always black or white. Come to terms with the gray areas of your life. It's OK if you make honest mistakes in judgment. We all do. One thing you can always do though, is recheck your thinking and recalibrate your thoughts. This process is fun and interesting. In everything, practice humility, be brave, develop moral stamina, and be careful about passing judgment on others.

Cultivate a Clean Mind
Canadian American sports coach and innovator James Naismith (1861–1939) admonished, "Be strong in body, clean in mind, lofty in ideals." These are goals we must all seek to emulate in life. The body is your temple, so treat it with respect and free yourself from fears both big and small. Discovering your weaknesses and acting on them calls for taking steps that will empower you. A person must be able to laugh at him- or herself. It was the novelist of *1984*, essayist, and journalist George Orwell (1903–1950), who believed, "Reality

exists in the human mind, and nowhere else." That's why having a clean mind is important for a healthy body.

Life's Transformation

A Christian believes that God is the beginning of his new birth—being born again in Christ we're a new creation endowed with wisdom. So, it's only right and just to depend solely on Christ. Jesus Christ is our provider and nourishment. Through him we can do all things, but we have to remember to always worship and praise him. Daily we have to pray for his guidance and that his will be done in our lives. Let your mind be at peace when you face trials and tribulations that come your way. A person may be able to do many things, but what's important is doing what's right and just. Approach your life as a special vocation by prayerfully seeking his guidance. Put your trust in the Lord, and he'll see to it that you'll receive your heart's desire. There is nothing in your life that he isn't aware of. So, your life's makeover has to start with acknowledging Jesus Christ as your Lord and Savior.

Thought of the Week

"Then the people answered, "Far be it from us that we should forsake the Lord to serve other gods...""

—Joshua 24:16 (NRSV)

Meditation 25

God's Time

Carl Sandburg (1878–1967), an American author and poet who won three Pulitzer Prizes, observed, "Time is the coin of your life. It is the only coin you have, and only you can determine how it will be spent. Be careful lest you let other people spend it for you." We must therefore approach the gift of time carefully and, wisely, and use it for good.

Making use of time in one's life can be tricky. Time, to most people is treated like a commodity. We agree that, "time is money." But it's a great deal more than that. To get another perspective, a person must only look at the saying, "To God, a thousand years are like one day." This is awesome! Then, the life span of man or woman can be likened to a grain of sand on a seashore.

Time is required for growth, development, and the production of materials, and commodities. Plants, like other living organisms, must have nutrients to grow, but this takes time. Growth and development may take a short or long period. After much dedication to being educated, a human mind has to grow in stages to learn vital lessons about living. It must also be fed with spiritual food in order to develop virtues of hope, faith and love.

Becoming very virtuous also takes time. Over a lifetime, a believer may have to faithfully study the New and Old Testaments to become spiritually active while learning to contribute to charitable causes. Over years he or she will spend much time being educated for his or her special vocation. To become proficient in a specialty to practice medicine, for example, a doctor may spend over six years in training and in internships.

Dreams and Aspirations

Growth and development will mean having dreams and aspirations. A student may have to imagine him- or herself doing a particular job. Does he have what it takes to do such a job? Is her ability suitable for her career choice? How will he do such a job? Is her personality right for her career choice? This is a time that calls for being honest with oneself. Over time, periods of discernment may lead to many ups and downs in one's life until one is able to settle on a true vocation.

Rejuvenation and Relaxation

With challenges on a job, there has to be breaks for rejuvenation and relaxation. That's the reason why most Americans take vacations. They have to be sure to have a good balance in their life and work. We may soon learn that our life may not be only for partying on such well-deserved breaks. The more Christian-minded personalities may decide that instead of lying on a beach on some exotic island sunbathing and drinking beer, it may be better for them to spend time helping build churches, repairing shelters in villages, or digging wells in some underdeveloped regions of a country.

Highly Effective People

In a book by Stephen R. Covey (1932–2012) entitled *The 7 Habits of Highly Effective People* which *Time* listed as one of the twenty-five most influential business-management books and which was a best seller that sold more than fifteen million copies in thirty-eight languages, Covey stressed, in "the seventh habit," having a "sustained, long-term, effective lifestyle." He encouraged his readers to "learn, commit, do," and envisioned they would find "personal freedom, security, wisdom and power." Such new realities could only be achieved by living a life true to God's time.

Thought of the Week

"For everything there is a season, and a time for every matter under heaven."

—Ecclesiastes 3:1 (NRSV)

Live with Dignity

Meditation 26

Live Wisely

L IVE WISELY AND with dignity—in the right way keep up with the Joneses. Seek real riches that are best for your interests. Look out for the best personalities to model your life after, and pay attention to what you're being fed by the media. Some things may be blessing or curses, so be fed wisely.

People may keep up with the Joneses in the wrong ways. Lifestyle is often a matter of choice, so be careful. Pay attention to the Joneses, but do not be attracted to their material possessions. Take note of the good things which they do. Are they respectable people? Are they fervent in their Christian walk? In time of need, could you depend on them to extend a helping hand? Do they flaunt their wealth? How do other neighbors and friends regard them? Make it your goal as a chance in a lifetime to emulate their good qualities. It was Irish playwright and founder of the London School of Economics George Bernard Shaw (1856–1950), who wrote, "Life isn't about finding yourself. Life is about creating yourself." Modeling and portraying what is best—that is the way you must begin, to create a new lifestyle from learning good things from the Joneses.

Alluring Desires

In life, there are alluring desires around every corner. A person only has to switch on any form of mass media and be bombarded with multiple images.

Whether it's the TV, computer, smartphone, or some social media, there to greet him or her is a myriad of good and bad pictures. Many visuals may be ads that seduce people by telling them how much better they will become if they use certain products. Sex, riches, beauty, speed and money are frequent themes in these pitches. It's wise for us to remember that the money and power that are portrayed so blatantly, are nothing more than false idols to be ignored. You have to be wise and move away from these choices that may harm you or your children. Pay particular attention to stay away from those products and issues that promote a self-centered lifestyle. Life is about helping people the right way and not selling them alcohol or an overabundance of products to drown out their sorrows.

Danish philosopher, theologian, and critic Soren Kierkegaard (1813–1855) observed, "Our life always expresses the result of our dominant thoughts." What we are fed will become the way we operate and value society. These things take center stage in our lives. So a proliferation of crime, disaster, betrayals, embezzlement, social revolutions, and wars will tend to capture our imagination and beliefs. Much worldly power is centered around atrocities and what we do to counter them. English Catholic historian, politician and writer Lord Acton (1834–1902) noted, "Power corrupts, and absolute power corrupts absolutely." It's wise therefore to avoid power-plays that corrupt our mind.

Defeat and Failure
Often an entanglement with worldly situations will lead to a run-in with the law. Any good citizen trapped in such a vicious cycle will be dishonored and his or her name will be dragged through the mud. We witness news reports about numerous crashes, bankruptcies, crime and violence. In the tourism industry, prostitution is alive, and this vice leads to the exacerbation of health issues. Through poor nutrition and lack of exercise people may experience the throes of life that contribute to many more health problems. People may lose hope about living because they are crushed by life's troubles––its pits and bogs. These are problems whereby living wisely and with dignity may enable

you to avoid such trouble. By taking positive steps you must actively work at anticipating and fending off defeat and failure in your life.

Climb a Mountain
When in a valley, set your eyes on a mountaintop. One good way to do this is to actively embrace Christian principles for living. In your life, accept our Lord and Savior, Jesus Christ. Let Jesus be your model in bearing your cross and in transforming you, for only through Christ will you be able to live wisely. He's the abundant One. With this new perspective, you'll view your life completely differently. Your life, renewed through faith in him, will undergo a conversion that will make you experience joys and sufferings like a saint.

American publisher and author William Feather (1889–1981) wrote, "One way to get the most out of life is to look upon it as an adventure." In your adventure, you'll live more compassionately, and when you depart from this world you'll enjoy eternal salvation. These things are the epitome of living a purpose-filled life with dignity, for you'll have ascended to the summit of the right and true mountain.

Thought of the Week
"Jesus said to him, "I am the way, and the truth, and the life. No one comes to the Father except through me.""

—John 14:6 (NRSV)

Meditation 27

Be the Best
How can you refine your personality? Some persons may think that you can do so by only taking care of your exterior. They may think one thing you must do is dress appropriately by wearing a suit when you sit in on important

meetings. You must don a tie, put on a piece of jewelry and wear a fashionable wrist watch to match. A religiously inclined person may display a necklace with a cross dangling on his or her chest. Other fashion-conscious dressers may pay attention to if their hair is black, brown or blond. To be sure, they are well-groomed; they may also wear a pair of the latest-style shoes. Such attire is beautiful and may strike some as having an air of respectability, however there's a lot more to being the best you can.

Much more is required to be the best. What about having a well-rounded education? Your goal should be to grow intellectually, physically and emotionally. With improved speech, you'll be able to score points. To be kind and courteous, are better goals. These human qualities will make you be like an actor in the world. You may want to view your personality as a mask of different colors. Ezra Pound's *Personnae* (1909) literally means "masks of actor," for we're basically actors on the world's stage. Some people may even consider their personality more favorably for they may be blessed with intelligence, cleverness, loveliness, or happiness. These gifts they may view as the essence of their blessedness.

Imperfections as Gifts
One thing is certain and that is we are all imperfect. By working hard to improve ourselves, we may still find that we are continually dogged by imperfections. One way in considering your attitude toward such defects is by viewing your imperfections as important gifts. Do not overly worry about them, but embrace them for what they really are. You may be suffering from alcoholism. What should you do? Recognize this affliction and take responsibility for it. Seek treatment, join Alcoholic Anonymous, and be open to family and friends about your disease. Share your story as a blessing in disguise, and see the stigma melt away from your consciousness. This gift that you once regarded in such a hateful way might well be the catalyst for helping other persons with a similar problem.

Through afflictions, some Christians and non-Christians alike have been known to develop a deeper love and understanding about God. In being an inspiration to others many saints have been able to mature more deeply in their faith. Cancer patients in remission may end up giving alms to other ailing patients at hospitals. They may view their newly found experiences as a vocation. Their outlook will inevitably become much more than coping with an ailment, which may appear gloomy and hopeless to many, but these patients may well discover that their service is valuable. We must always praise these sufferers and their commitments to other ailing patients. Their service must be applauded for people will find hope, encouragement and strength through their dedication.

There are some who may view having imperfections as a bad thing. American comedian, actor, and writer of the TV series *"Roseanne,"* Carrie Snow observed, "Technology…is a queer thing. It brings you great gifts with one hand, and it stabs you in the back with the other." Could she be referring to the faces of media—good and bad? In the media we may learn about some leaders' glorious achievements and contributions and after awhile their names are being dragged through mud by the same commentators who were praising them. In media and in life, we're presented with the good, bad and indifferent, but the wise will still learn from these situations. Technology, whether it is radio, TV, cable or the Internet has its imperfections, but should still be viewed as a gift—imperfect gifts though they may be. God-fearing people will always benefit from what's best in the media.

With Care and Respectability

Why must we be flippant connivers? We are entrusted at birth with a myriad of gifts. Even a person who is brain-damaged has gifts to share with us. The tramp who may be ignored is also gifted. In God's providence, we are his caretakers. We dislike criminals running rampantly in our cities and will do anything to stop them. Why not do away with jealousies we often foster about others? Do not be too upset about situations you can't control, for God is always in control. At times life can be more than a struggle, but we're blessed with grace and goodness to see this struggle through. In life a lot of situations are not as menacing as they appear. They only call for prayer, understanding and handling with commonsense. In our challenging lifestyles we must promote honest values and morals when facing the world.

To refine your personality laugh a lot and be good-humored about the little and big things. With fortitude and persistence, you'll touch what is truly authentic in life. By being a Good Samaritan, you can help the less fortunate and focus your eyes on our Good Shepherd—our Lord and Savior, Jesus Christ. Humans are basically good. Good can mean holy too, as in Good Friday—the Friday preceding Easter, the anniversary of Jesus's crucifixion. Allow Christ to refine your personality, and you'll touch the essence of being whole. So when you sit down for a meal each and every day, and on Good Friday, you'll do so in commemoration of the day of the Lord's Supper, for you can only become the best through Him.

Thought of the Week

"...in him was life, and the life was the light of all people."

—John 1:4 (NRSV)

Meditation 28

Sky Is the Limit

Are you reluctant to give love or do you nurture feelings of ill will? It may be that you are harboring a grudge. That's when you can't budge from sad thoughts about life. Why aren't you able to move on from these twisted ways? It sure sounds like the sludge that is a grudge. There's a song by a British quintet entitled, "A Grudge in the Key of Sludge," which was released on July 29, 2013 that captured a rather melancholy state.

Blood, Sweat and Tears

Some may come to view life as nothing more than blood, sweat and tears. True, there can be hard times when working and struggling to accomplish goals. As the saying goes, "No pain, no gain." Often we make sacrifices in putting our hands to the wheel and laboring at tasks. These tasks may not necessarily be physical, but can include any type of work. Studying, for example, to receive an education, is challenging. Some students may fear taking courses that are too difficult. These may be in science. Yet, there are those who may love science and technology. Others may struggle with a physical activity, English, or a foreign language. But through it all, do we have to feel as though we're ill-suited for the rigors of life? We don't have to.

There's an American jazz-rock group – called Blood, Sweat, and Tears, that was well known in the 1960s and early 1970s. It was a brainchild of the legendary Al Kooper, who put a new spin on the group's name, for it brought joy with music. Songs that were great hits were, "Child Is the Father to the Man," "And When I Die," "You Made Me So Very Happy," and "Spinning Wheel." Their music and lyrics captured the realities of life. In short, they assure us, "One time you're up, another you're down. Now you're happy, soon you're sad. Anyway, life's never the same." So, why then will you want to hold on to feelings of ill-will?

Untapped Creativity
Sooner or later in life you'll find your niche. Scripture assures us that every one of us has at least one gift. Some Christians may be blessed with many more. The key to unlocking your hidden potential is to filter out the noise and distraction from your life. With patience, embrace peace and quiet when tackling problems. Avoid situations that make you unfocused and irritable, and deal sensibly with those who are hurtful. Play music that will lighten your mood and cultivate fruitful qualities that are beneficial to you. With prayer and meditation, trust your own experiences and you'll surely discover your untapped potential.

Taste Life's Possibilities
Pursue your own fulfillment—peace, joy and comfort. Find abundance by observing signs that come your way and test your beliefs. In this quest, you'll be sure to encounter the miraculous. By accessing the unknown areas in your life, you'll be able to sleep better, have more energy and be at peace.

Concerning future guidance, you'll probably need essential information from a trusted mentor. But as you grow older and wiser, you'll realize that although work and money are important, life consists of other more important things—especially small things that you were overlooking all along. In a British documentary entitled, *"The Possibilities Are Endless"*, which was released on November 7, 2014, and starred Edwyn Collins and William Collins, focused on life's infinite realities which was most revealing. Watching a film like this one can be helpful.

Why Bear a Grudge When the Sky Is the Limit?

Being reluctant to give should never be in the playbook of Christians. They must reach out to the needy and to everyone else. The essence of Christian living is to give and serve freely with joy. Through their talent and treasure some Christians are avid givers. They volunteer at hospitals, nursing homes, book mobiles and libraries. When it comes to treasure, it isn't only the collection plate in which they drop checks on Sundays, but they donate to other charitable organizations as well.

In giving, there should be no ill will. Indeed, Christians see themselves as being truly blessed. For many years, they have worked in careers and are giving back to their community. They consider these acts as God-given, for they have tasted life's possibilities and are happy to reciprocate. Such giving is wonderful, because it provides vital needs to the least among us. It's true that the life saved, may well become a shining light for us to emulate. So be sure, to keep sharing abundantly. Live peaceably with happiness in your heart, for the sky is the limit.

Thought of the Week

"And God saw that light was good; and God separated the light from darkness."

—Genesis 1:4 (NRSV)

Meditation 29

Touch Lives

Four-time Grammy Award winner and singer-songwriter Tracy Chapman (b. 1964) observed, "I have seen and met angels wearing the disguise of ordinary people living ordinary lives." Much can be said about the simplicity of angels. These are the people we take for granted and by not making a fuss about them. They go about their business with an unexplained urgency. Their business is helping people. Divinely inspired, their walk among mortals is viewed as special. You can find them feeding the hungry, comforting the poor, clothing the naked, and housing the homeless. Just regard this quote from Mother Teresa (1910–1997), Blessed of Calcutta, Roman Catholic sister, "We can do no great things—only small things with great love."

Small Things of Great Love

By 2012, in some 133 countries Mother Teresa was known to direct 4,500 sisters. Her mission of charity is alive among the helpless of the world. She had been in the slums of Calcutta tending to those with HIV/AIDS, leprosy and tuberculosis, and was prominent in providing soup kitchens, dispensaries, clinics, family counseling, orphanages, and schools to benefit the poor.

Mother Teresa was undoubtedly a beacon amongst us. She shined her light on many of the most rejected people in India. Adherents of her charity have followed in her footsteps. The need amongst the tens of millions around the globe continues to be great. Their demand increases yearly, as the worldwide population grows at an alarming rate in India, China, and on the continents of Africa and South America.

Throw Off Your Old Skin

Snakes, salamanders and frogs shed their skins regularly. For these species, such shedding is a sign of growth and development. Humans too, do a different kind of shedding. Their shedding can be viewed metaphorically. This may be seen as spiritual growth—changing from the "old you" to a "new you." Such life brings with it a vitality that is spiritually, physically, and emotionally sound. It can be seen in an awareness of how we interact with the least amongst us. Loving them like our neighbors and embracing their families is a way of shedding our "old skin."

Care for the Destitute

In a variety of fields, some professionals have used their calling to help others. But, are we doing enough? It's like Christ to feed the poor, to clothe the naked and to care for the destitute. Such an attitude means taking up a lifestyle of service and dedication of which there are a few outstanding role models. It's good to have an outlook like Dr. Jonas Salk (1914–1995), developer of a vaccine against the crippling disease of polio when he remarked, "I feel the greatest reward for doing is the opportunity to do more." Dr. Salk was pursuing the goal of finding a vaccination for HIV/AIDS when he died. His life work was a culmination of years of dedication to painstaking research.

Our work in the world calls for many hands at the wheel. Planet earth is crying out in pain, and Christians have to pick up their crosses and follow Christ, his apostles and saints. These were all shining lights in a broken world, weighed down by sin, abuse, drought, famine, war and disease. As Americans, we may not be presently experiencing afflictions like some of our brothers and sisters in other countries, but it is wise for us to always remember the dire adversities that exist throughout our home - - earth. Let us give a helping hand when and where we can.

Thought of the Week

"He raises up the poor from the dust; he lifts up the needy from the ash heap, to make them sit with princes and inherit a seat of honor. For the pillars of the earth are the Lord's, and on them he has set the world."

—1 Samuel 2:8 (NRSV)

Cultural Attributes

American Culture

AMERICANS LIVE IN a fast-paced society. We're used to a 24/7 news cycle with instant news updates. Media conglomerates promote "web speed" for professionals and all other Americans alike. Internet surfers become impatient if websites take long to load. On social media there are millions who participate in the minute by minute snapshots of life. On multiple TV channels, images move fast and change rapidly. Audiences are bombarded with sound bites, which are entertaining to watch, but do not tell the whole story. News stories are presented in fifteen-or thirty-second segments like commercials. Such fare is backed up with weekly polling and telephone interviews to monitor the public's sentiments.

Radio and TV call-in talk shows demand answers right away, and they give callers quick feedback about education, religion, the economy, health and disasters. Much information is sent by pictures via i-Phones. Americans have become used to cutting corners, logging on, tuning in and dialing up for services. We live in an age of instant gratification. By pressing a few buttons, some people use the Grindr app on their smartphones to find potential dates.

Around the nation, millions instantly stream videos. DVDs come from Netflix, which has more than eight million mail subscribers. Many shoppers receive services on the same day, and there are self-check lines in stores that keep customers moving. Walmart has Walmart-To-Go, Amazon has expedited shopping, and Americans are used to fast foods with drive through-windows at McDonald's, Hardee's and Wendy's.

Quick-fix Mediocrity

Some critics say that quick fixes may result in nimble thinking. Some educators think learning takes time and repetition by students to really get it. Americans appear presently convinced that "snail mail" is out when they can email friends and coworkers and use instant messaging. Many consumers have become used to paying a bit more for overnight shipping.

America has become a society of texting and tweeting. Some social media platforms accept no more than 140 characters per tweet. Whatever you have to say, say it fast and in a sound bite. To some, dating is speed dating. No longer is it required to know a person for awhile, before deciding to date. Gadgets and more gadgets have become the name of the game. It was actor, writer and director David Duchovny (b. 1960), who felt, "I'm kind of stupid when it comes to gadgets." Was he saying that he has allowed gadgets to rule his life? Or, does he mean that he's stupid when it comes to knowing what gadgets can really do?

Speed with Emptiness

Since everything is happening so fast, it leaves us wondering what's next. In trying to multitask, are we forming bad habits of dependency on gadgets? Does our impatience in demanding things now, lead to health problems, such as diabetes, high blood pressure and obesity, because we rely on fast food and soda machines? Must we blame capitalism and consumerism for dishing out what we want faster and faster? How must a person view his or her dependency on new technological devices? This is a tricky problem.

A False Sense of Security

It was record producer, conductor and twenty-seven-time Grammy winner Quincy Jones (b. 1933), who observed, "I have all the tools and gadgets. I tell my son, who's a producer, 'You never work for the machine; the machine works for you.'" Is this the lesson we must take away about inventions that keep speeding up our lives? Should it be said then, that Americans should pick and choose from the technological offerings that work best for them? But, aren't they failing at this?

Christian Insights of Developments

To a Christian, being wise must be key in making decisions about his or her nation's culture. Patience is a virtue, but society's growing impatience may be a bad thing, if not checked. Despite the rate of speed everywhere, a believer may be concerned that Americans are heading down a road of chaos. It must always be remembered that God is in control. Why must a person allow his mind and body to deteriorate from mental health issues, because of the demands placed on him by gadgets that are promoted as helping him or her? This is when a believer has to live in the world and be not of this world.

A Christian must learn to cultivate patience—the capacity to endure hardship, difficulty or inconvenience without complaint. Daily devotion is essential for every Christian. Reflecting and praying for wisdom will help a seeker of God's grace to embrace the fruits of the spirit. In dedication to the Lord, he or she'll come to know peace, love, joy and fulfillment, even when it appears that his world is steadily spinning out of control. Instant gratification will never be the answer for his or her security in understanding life's problems. We have to live and face life's issues through perseverance and by meeting difficulties when they arise. One of the tests of our modern age is how to live victoriously in a fast-paced nation. This challenge ought to be met head on, by making wise choices about living a Christian lifestyle in America.

Thought of the Week

"I will make of you a great nation, and I will bless you, and make your name great, so that you will be a blessing."

—Genesis 12:2 (NRSV)

Meditation 31

Life's Remote

Need a remote? Do you think that by having one you can control your life? It may be natural to think so—if you can control your mind, you may be able to solve your problems. But, is that possible?

Personal Control

In thinking about oneself, it's usually a battle with the mind. You may try to control your thoughts like using a TV remote. But what should you think about? "Use commonsense" you say, "for I'll have a perfect plan." By encouraging good thoughts—those that are enlightening to the body, mind and spirit—you'll be able to solve many of your problems. These must be the ones you feed and nurture. Then, by starving thoughts that are negative you'll be able to discourage unwanted feelings. Do breathing exercises, meditate and pray for total control. Do such techniques work? Yes, to some extent. These negative thoughts you may capture and run out of your mind, but other emotional ones may linger.

Controlling Your Emotions

Psychologists warn us about the consequences of feeding our mind with negative thoughts. When they come to your mind, do something about them. Try distracting yourself by going for a walk and playing music you like. You'll surely change your thinking. If negative emotions persist, do not dwell on them, but pray to be free from them. Call on the Lord, quote Scriptures, refresh your mind, and watch a change in attitude come over you.

Dream Dreams

A dreamer may dream about the future. It's estimated that 20 percent of the population are lucid dreamers. Another 50 percent occasionally remember some of their dreams. These are dreams while asleep, but we're all dreamers when we're awake and active. Dreaming is like hitting the remote to be transported to an imaginary place. The only thing is, your remote doesn't actually present you with an experience like the movies.

Rewinding Your Life

Unlike the VHS tapes that were once popular, our lives cannot be rewound. Listen to what Frank Matobo from Africa University, Zimbabwe, noticed, "Time waits for no man. A second of doubt means you are a second behind. So make a choice use it wisely or lose it forever. There is simply no rewind." This is why a believer must have faith in the Lord Jesus Christ. He must embrace life, believe in good things and accentuate the positive. A Christian must never doubt but always accept what's holy, true, just and honest. These attributes come with perseverance in his beliefs and studying the Word. There's a Facebook community where people want to rewind their lives. They can only speculate about those things that they wish to change, have not done, and if they had a chance to do it over again, what they would do differently.

Fast-Forward through Problems

Like with the rewind feature, individuals can use their mind to recall past events. They can linger on certain experiences, errors and faulty thinking of the past, but with the fast-forward button they can only use his imagination to dream. We are incapable and limited for we can't fast-forward our minds through problems. We'll never be able to know fully what the future will bring. With a movie you can speed forward and find out, because all scenes are already prerecorded. You can watch the end, or middle before the beginning. In real life, you can only have this feature imaginatively. That's why Christians can focus on eternal life, because they have discerned, pictured and are reassured by the biblical promises that their commitment in the Lord and Savior, Jesus Christ is sound. Indeed, this is through faith, for they have been exposed to the totality of God's Word.

Pause and Mute Buttons

In life, some critics will argue that there's never pause and mute buttons through which we have control. From birth, the play button propels us on our trajectory. It's for us to steer our ship and do our best to avoid shipwrecks. Let us reflect on what author Sonya Parker knew, "Life doesn't come with a rewind, fast-forward or pause button. Once it starts it plays until it ends or until you press stop."

It'll be of interest if we can view the pause and mute buttons as times for reflection, peace and quiet in life. Being caught up in a hectic schedule sometimes it's best to be able to withdraw to a quiet place, close our eyes and pray to God. Our prayer can very well be on pause, when we fail to utter words and are one with all creation. It's suicide or murder if you hit the stop button. Never do it, but let life end naturally and you'll be blessed.

Thought of the Week

"And he said, "Hear my words: When there are prophets among you, I the Lord make myself known to them in visions; I speak to them in dreams.""

—Numbers 12:6 (NRSV)

Meditation 32

Lies and Fear

Knowingly and unknowingly we're all guilty of telling lies. Exodus 20:16 (NRSV) tells us "You shall not bear false witness against your neighbor.". An original song entitled "Don't Lie to Me" performed by Phillip Lucero and Jessie Farren was prominently featured in a music video. Episodes of an American crime drama on the Fox network were popular from 2009 to 2011. The show was called "Lie to Me". Lies appear in different guises in many world-wide cultures. On this TV show "Lie to Me", the Lightman Group accepted assignments from local and federal law enforcement agencies to assist in their investigations. Their group endeavored to find the truth through interpreting impressions through a Facial Action Coding System (FACS) and body language.

People Lie
To cover their tracks, lies are used by criminal and non-criminal minds. People use deception, often to save their neck, or in trying to get out of a troubling situation. Some individuals may feel that lying may make them look good or better than others, so they fabricate stories to present themselves in a good light. Some will come to see what they are doing is false and despise these deeds.

By withholding vital pieces of information about themselves or situations, these deceivers may think their spin on things may not make them look bad. Such lies of omissions are generally practiced by politicians, salesmen or even friends. During wartime nations may broadcast propaganda meant to give them a boost in the "war of words."

Lies can also be made through ignorance. Persons may be certain of details about a current affairs issue, for example. They may not see the whole picture because they are convinced that they are right. Through sheer ignorance they may be making decisions by giving their company's line, but it may be untrue. Yet they continually insist that their decisions are right. This information may be unknown on the part of the agents, due to lack of understanding the whole situation.

People, Fear and Lies
It can well be that people actually lie because they may fear the consequences of their actions. They may feel that if they tell the truth they may get into trouble, so they suppress the truth about some matter. Liars twist the facts in order to wiggle out of uncomfortable situations. It was President Franklin D. Roosevelt (1882–1945) who remarked, "The only thing to fear is fear itself."

On December 10, 1948, the United Nations General Assembly referred to freedom from fear - as a fundamental human right, being one of the "four freedoms in its charter. Whether it is fear of the build up of armaments or cheating, we must always be courageous and tell the truth.

It is quite important to be brave, for in 1943 Norman Rockwell (1894–1978) created *Freedom from Fear,* a series of paintings called *Four Freedoms.* This theme was prominent in David M. Kennedy's book, *Freedom from Fear.* Even in times of national crisis when disinformation and propaganda rule the airwaves, Americans must never fear, for with courage, freedom and hope, the truth will always prevail.

Live to the Fullest
Let's forget lies and embrace love which leads to self-esteem and self-confidence. Come to know the Lord and Savior, Jesus Christ who provides for us from his abundance. This calls for trusting in a supreme being. With this belief, every fabrication will cease for we will now be focused on him. If believers are determined to achieve a goal, they will now persevere to the end by doing what's right, true and just.

Individuals will be able to concentrate on what dreams are most important to them, which will determine the way they live. Given a life free from lies and deception, they will stop judging themselves and cast their nets into the water. Not heeding the frustration about not catching any fish, at the Lord's command, they will cast their net again into the deep, and won't believe their catch.

Thought of the Week
"Yea, though I walk through the valley of the shadow of death, I will fear no evil: for Thou art with me; Thy rod and Thy staff they comfort me."

—Psalm 23:4 (KJV)

Meditation 33

In the Fast Lane

"Life in the Fast Lane" was a song written by Joe Walsh, Glenn Frey and Don Henley. But, such a life is a rather risky way of living. Some may see it as exciting, but what's required is often dangerous. It's lifestyle and adherents are often the rich and well-to-do.

Such a lifestyle is symbolic of our pop culture with its lyrics about sex that are often lewd. Much of this fare tells about wealth and social status, so prominently displayed by some Hollywood stars, their adherents and admirers. Actors are seen as having women in compromising situations. The use of recreational drugs is considered a status symbol, and many film and TV idols are in scenes that glorify sex and violence.

This glamorization extends to depictions of dandy men and flashy women who go to fabulous parties and drive fancy cars. These individuals are representative of the jet age, flying for engagements to and from New York, London and Paris. They rub shoulders with elites and splurge at expensive hotels. This lifestyle will strike many observers as being seductive and enticing.

Often there are salacious stories of such personalities in the *National Enquirer, Star Magazine*, and the *Daily Mirror*. But what about their behavior and their potential effects on children? To a child's impressionable mind such a lifestyle is tempting and dangerous. Children may come away thinking that's how rich and famous people live. Some may imitate their idol's speech, dress and behavior. The effects may well result in becoming juvenile delinquents, being promiscuous, and living selfish lives if they are not careful.

Slow Down and Think

A good reality check is getting to know the Lord and having these so called "beautiful people" change their way of life. Families must reflect on matters of the spirit and turn off the TV, if shows aren't appropriate for children to watch. Be more selective and let the family watch shows that are edifying and uplifting to the spirit. They ought to resist the temptations of the flesh that lead to tragedies and death. A household must make it a habit to meditate on the "Word of God", which brings peace, hope and joy to a household.

Adults must set the example for their children. They ought to pray with their children when seeking guidance and discernment from the Holy Spirit. In so doing, parents will better be able to select those physical activities and games that are wholesome for their kids to play. They will learn about appropriate entertainment for their family, and will set limits for living within the boundaries of a God-fearing lifestyle.

Take Back Your Lives
In following these simple steps of advocacy, parents will be able to take back their lives that they have unwittingly surrendered to evil forces. Their actions will trigger a feeling of hopefulness when they begin to experience the goodness of God. Their children will be blessed, cherished and nurtured to live according to what's best for them. These will be aims and goals of living in a blessed and sacred home that will be beneficial to their family's future.

Thought of the Week
"For the Lamb which is in the midst of the throne shall feed them, and shall lead them unto living fountains of waters: and God shall wipe away all tears from their eyes."

—Revelation 7:17 (KJV)

Meditation 34

Seeds of Hope
What are you sowing? By what you do, are you sowing seeds of peace, love, joy, hope, and tranquility? Is your goal to love your neighbor as yourself? Do

you feed the hungry and house the homeless? Are you an advocate for the least among us? Episcopal Relief & Development (ERD) is doing these things. They have trained some 930,000 volunteers for ERD's NetsforLife, which is active in developing countries.

ERD has brought their services to:

- Liberia where agricultural priorities are practiced;
- Yangon, Myanmar through the Anglican Men's Association (AMA) with demonstrations of small holder farms;
- Nicaragua where malnourished children are fed soy flour mixed with corn flour;
- Nyanza in Kisuma, Kenya, where there is a 95 percent HIV-negative graduation rate for children;
- Gaza Province of Mozambique where the inhabitants make bricks to sell and build their own homes; and the Diocese of Tamale where there are education, seeds, fertilizers and an increase in crops.

Give Back to the Universe
What ERD is doing, according to their 2015 Lenten Meditations, is giving back to society in education, skill, love, and training. Are you doing the same with your talent and treasure? You may have benefited through scholarships from a university. Are you dedicated to doing charitable work? Like thousands of these volunteers, the poor, hungry, and homeless are depending on you.

Give Joyfully
It's good to be a happy giver. As a charitable donor, it's a gift to have a sense of humor to share with those you meet. A human touch will put a smile on someone's face. Sharing in such an undertaking will enlighten a recipient through knowing that you care and are giving from your heart. Your attitude will be positive. Some givers make jokes, are friendly, and the

receivers of their gifts are happy to be with them. It beats being negative and depressed as though you're carrying the burden of tens of millions needy on your shoulders.

Whether it is through the Diocese of El Salvador, which provides services and training to many, or being an advocate for the over fifty thousand unaccompanied children from Central America that cross the U.S. Border, play your part in creating a future for the least among us. The seeds you sow will send roots deep down into the soil of hopefulness. Remembering that you're mainly a branch of that eternal vine is an apt way of focusing your care. But through faithfulness, you'll make it possible for your branch to bear fruit in abundance, so that when the harvest comes you'll be awarded your just reward. For more information, ERD's website can be accessed at: <www.episcopalrelief.org>.

Thought of the Week
"Thou shalt fear the Lord thy God, and serve Him, and shalt swear by His name."

—Deuteronomy 6:13 (KJV)

Meditation 35

Worn Out
Are you a damaged human being with ailments? Do you have constant headaches, low energy, aches, pains, and tense muscles, or are you nervous with colds and sweating palms? Are you going about with clenched jaws and grinding your teeth? Do you suffer from palpitations, anxiety attacks, ulcers and have violent outbursts? Do you suffer from a mental problem, an eating disorder, or are you obese? Then you may well be worn out by the demands of the world.

You may have a lack of appetite and be hooked on alcohol, drugs, or nicotine. Maybe you pace, fidget, and are unable to settle down. With this behavior, you can't marshal your thoughts to focus on your job. You may even have other afflictions of chronic diseases e.g., diabetes, high blood pressure, chronic renal failure, or congestive heart failure. These may well be symptoms that show you are burned out and overloaded.

Other symptoms may be that you are not sleeping well at night, have no sexual drive, and no longer have interests besides work. Your condition can all be due to the rat-race that you find yourself a part of. Constantly popping pills and, suffering from frequent infections, you can't seem to keep away from the doctor's office.

A Competitive Spirit

From childhood you were taught to be competitive. "Be the best you can. The sky is the limit." You never knew it, but you were coerced by adults and peers in joining the bandwagon of competitors. You're now working in overdrive—sixteen hours per day, and hooked on technological devices for quick results. You can't even find time to sit down and enjoy a book. Although you may be overweight and have bad eating habits, physical activities are no longer part of your daily routine. You failed to take the warning from quotation anthologist Terri Gullemets (b. 1973), who said, "If your teeth are clenched and your fists are clenched, your lifespan is probably clenched." Now you're paying the price.

Be Happy Again

It was British philosopher Bertrand Russell (1872–1970), who observed, "One of the symptoms of an approaching nervous breakdown is the belief that one's work is terribly important." You have always felt this way about work and there's a price for keeping up with the Joneses. Your life is in disarray and you realize it's time to slow down and start smelling the roses—what is left of them.

Your first step is to continue seeing your doctor for treatment of your afflictions, eating healthily, exercising every day, being sure to rest and relax, and taking medications as prescribed. You must also receive counseling, but remember not to keep God out of the picture. Start praying for healing and guidance, for he'll be of comfort and provide for your needs. You'll find that knowing our Lord and Savior, Jesus Christ will bring peace, joy, love and hope. It's not that you'll no longer have problems but that with spiritual awakening, Jesus will be your companion, defender and protector.

Christians do suffer. Some saints suffer willingly for redemptive purposes, but others have prayed for healing and were healed. It'll be important in your Christian walk to bring all matters—good and bad—, before the Lord for his blessings.

It is only then, your life will begin to take on new dimensions you never really dreamed of. It'll be a new and purpose-driven life. Remember - in the ways of the world, we were never meant to be competitive. In the Lord's eyes we're all equal. Talent is in every part of one's body. An eye can't say to a foot, "I'm worth more that you." We're all important and talented in our own God-given way. This is one thing you'll discover while living the correct way in order to be successful.

Thought of the Week
"Desire not the night, when people are cut off in their place."

—Job 36:20 (KJV)

Meditation 36

Small but Beautiful
It's always best to embrace small and beautiful growth. This means that consumers will have to downsize when pursuing a more spiritual lifestyle. There must not only be a focus on producing personal desires but on the right type

of goals as well. An accumulation of more material possessions is far from the answer. Overabundance can lead to all sorts of dehumanization, so we must ask, "What's the reason for acquiring earthly possessions?"

As caretakers of planet earth we have ownership over many acquisitions. It's for us not to be greedy by living a gluttonous life. We must be good stewards by making what has been bequeathed to us our responsibility to preserve and protect. We must be sure this ownership doesn't lead us to clutter and pollute our environment. On our minds, must always be ecological concerns. We can then be defenders of people's rights by endeavoring to protect our environment.

Our Usage of Commodities
Our production model must be geared toward the purposeful usage of commodities. It's for us to concentrate on what we essentially want and not delight in an overabundance of material things or to merely be pleasure seekers in the world. Ask the question, "When is enough, enough?" It'll be necessary to look at your belongings and consider what you can do without. In their twilight years many seniors find it necessary to downsize their homes.

Notable writers have opted for living a simple life. These individuals are showing us how to make the earth more sustainable. These authors, philosophers, social scientists and media critics include Ernest Callenbach, Duane Elgin, Richard Gregg, Harland Hubbard, Mark Boyle, Jim Herkel and Daniel Suelo. By living simple lives these individuals are respecting the environment in which they live. They are living based on what their daily needs are but not through extravagance.

Media for Sustainability
Print media like *Mother Earth News*, *The Power of Half* and *The Good Life* have been pushing us toward this simplicity with their repeated mantra of living according to our needs. If possible, it'll be wise to go back to the land, for it's amazing how much the New and Old Testaments tell us about a pastoral lifestyle and nature. Psalm 23 (NRSV) aptly describes us as "sheep with a

shepherd." It envisions a future of everlasting joy, peace, humility and abiding grace by loving God.

A British economist E.F. Schumacher's *Small is Beautiful* shows us the right type of growth required. This growth must also be spiritual in nature. We have to put our trust in the Lord and develop the right attitude about what lifestyle is really required. In short, we have to pray for guidance to make the right decisions about our living conditions. Knowledge, wisdom and truth must always be pursued when making decisions about nature.

Small is Beautiful in the *Times Literary Supplement* was considered among the one hundred most influential books. But "spiritual growth" will help us to more fully understand why God is asking us to embrace simplicity. Such simplicity will provide insights about our lives, needs, hopes and dreams. In the end it'll help us to be better and better stewards, not only of our households, but of all God's creation.

Blessings from God
Our lives will be blessed if we live God-centered lives. Each day, we'll be able to give thanks not only for the food we eat, the clothes we wear, and our homes, but also for changes of our ways. Simplicity will be natural for we'll feed the poor and hungry, and provide for the homeless. They too are our neighbors whom we often leave out of our abundance. Doing these things with a willing heart will enable us to be truly blessed because we'll be living God-directed lives. Once they are accomplished, we shall proclaim ourselves adherents of the right way in pursuing small but beautiful growth.

Thought of the Week
"So shall the king greatly desire thy beauty: for He is thy Lord; and worship thou Him."

—Psalm 45:11 (KJV)

Our Real Home

Your Earthly Journey

H ow's your earthly journey? Where will you end up? In the Middle Ages, it was believed that there was paradise on earth. This place was described as having perfect beauty, peace and immortality. Such an ideal place was believed to be located in the Near East. It was considered to be the Garden of Eden that the Bible tells us about in the book of Genesis. This garden was said to be never destroyed with the fall of man.

In William Morris' *Earthy Paradise* was a collection of narrative poems that dealt in its prologue about the flight of Norse sailors from the Black Death and their search for an earthly paradise. But daily, Americans in their journey are involved with everyday realities. Some are known to attend school for years, have careers, be affiliated with a religious group, have families and friends, meet strangers and experience a diversity of cultures. Most Christians believe in life after death, but there are some non- believers who don't know what to expect from life. Regardless of our beliefs, we're all on a journey and we know we'll eventually die. Christians believe that after death they will rise again and reside in heaven.

Right Comfort

Americans wish to journey quickly and comfortably. There are a lot of devices that are promoted in our stores to accomplish these ends. Consumers use right services, right chairs, and adjustable mechanisms, or they stay in comfortable hotels.

They wish to sleep right and improve their home efficiency by having comfort in every room. Some may use a Geothermal Unit and have satellite TV programs that are easily accessed and convenient; ride a hybrid or comfort bike-shopper for moving comfort when buying groceries. With these comforts, they are all moving rapidly along in style as some will proudly say. But where are we going? Where will we end up?

Walking Without a Destination

It seems to some folks that are journeying that they don't appear to have any clear destination in mind. Many take flights with their imagination and may even descend to the underworld. This has been the motif of many stories in mythology and folklore. In such stories, a descent is generally made to capture an abducted person, or someone who has died. It's also to seize treasure, or to discover secrets about the rulers of the underworld. Myths like these appear in Greek, Jewish, Slavic, Hindu, Chinese and Japanese mythology.

We don't even have to reflect mentally about folklore, for today many of these circumstances are played out in real life. Persons journeying are involved in chases, crime, burglaries, interludes, drama, fiction, murder, assassinations, discoveries, and a myriad of situations involving intrigue. Through our diverse vocations we takes trips along different avenues in our lives. "Where?" Some may ask. It seems everywhere, in all directions, doing good and bad. Nevertheless scripture is clear, the kingdom of heaven is won by the faithful through grace. Some worldly and bad characters will surely end up in the same place with reasonably good men and women who have tried to live respectable lives.

Your Inner Voice

Our inner voice seems to be on a journey of its own. Often it praises us for successes we enjoy. Then, there's disillusionment. Some situations may seem bizarre and we wonder where we're heading. At other times, our psyche assures us that we're right to be happy, maybe because we've won a scholarship to a prestigious university, or have been honored as man or woman of the year by *Time* magazine. In our mind's eye, we can picture the accolades. Having reflected on how blessed we are, we thank our stars for our good fortune.

Your inner voice may take other flights. As you're journeying you reason how conscientious you've been at work. Having no reservations about your thoughts, you seem encouraged about some good people in the world. Soon dissolution creeps in. You start doubting what you really believe. You feel now you deserve more from life. People you observe are not treating you as kindly as you think they should. Your feelings are now interspersed with anxiety attacks, but why? To you, these seem to reveal some basic need that you can't quite put your finger on. You've to have friends—, colleagues with whom you can talk and share some of your innermost thoughts.

You have tried a psychiatrist, for example, but that doesn't seem to help the way you wish. Your thinking directs you to latch on to a Christian friend to help find answers that appear to be evading you. This you'll try first before seeing your man of the cloth, for counseling. In church, you find yourself surrounded by Christian love and you did discover in your Christian friend, a gem who you met at Barnes & Noble. She's pious, goodhearted and strikes you as having a happy disposition. Your thoughts have now started to be peaceful as you journey on, for you have found what you see as real peace and happiness. This is through his or her kindness and how he respects and treats you as a person. You reasoned, it's not fame or fortune that matters most, but contentment and inner-happiness. You presently believe, "I'm set in life and ready for God's kingdom."

Thought of the Week
"And the Lord said unto Satan, Whence cometh thou? Then Satan answered the Lord, and said, From going to and fro in the earth, and from walking up and down in it."

—Job 1:7 (KJV)

Meditation 38

Our Eternal Soul

American author, political activist and lecturer Helen Keller (1880–1968) felt, "Character cannot be developed in ease and quiet. Only through experience of trial and suffering can the soul be strengthened, ambition inspired, and success achieved." Developing this necessary character is seen as crucial for our soul's development. A person's soul generally goes through trials and tribulations that serves as a catalysts for successful growth and development.

Our Soul Weighed Down

Many persons are weighed down by problems. At times, during this earthly pilgrimage their souls experience torment. During these moments an individual may dialogue with his or her soul. Such conversation is one of uncertainty, skepticism, and denial. Compromises are made that may be troubling, many of which, he or she may live to regret. By feeding on the evil that bombards our psyche, our actions may have the result of us having weakened souls. That's why we sing hymns and talk about our wretched souls. It's greatly feared that when continuing down a perilous path we'll lose our soul.

What Is the Soul?

In Hebrew scripture, the soul and the body are not sharply distinguished. The rabbis of the Talmudic period recognize a separation of body and soul. In Genesis, God is known to have breathed a soul into the first man, Adam. From that beginning, the soul was viewed as a separate entity from the body. Christians place their trust in a soul that will live on when they die. Following in the footsteps of Jesus Christ, they look forward to the resurrection after death.

A soul shares its earthly life with the body. Judaism like Christianity believes in the soul's immortality. Greek philosopher Plato (428/427 or 424/423–348/347 BC) taught about this immortality of the soul while Christians believe that there would be an embodied resurrection as found in scripture. Greek philosopher Aristotle (384–322 BC) reasoned somewhat differently from Plato when he stressed that the soul was the human being.

Italian Catholic and Dominican theologian Thomas Aquinas (1225–1274) promoted his view of an individual's immortality. Since 1869, it became the Roman Catholic position that our soul is conferred at the moment of conception. Presently this is regarded as an inviolable truth by the Catholic Church.

Feed Your Soul
It is imperative that we strive to have a peaceful soul fed by the good things in life. In our worldly journey, a person's soul cannot be left alone to be heavily burdened with evil. By embracing what is pure, just, and honorable, some tormented souls will be healed through prayer and meditation. In this way, humans will profit in growing and developing spiritually. Be respectful to your soul by practicing the virtues of love, joy, faith and peace. These attributes will rejuvenate and refresh your being.

The Kingdom of Soul
During Mass Christians may discover the precious kingdom of the soul. Within the inner recesses of their being they will be spiritually filled. This will be achieved in a church that is God-centered. In practice and with faith, a believer will be able to cultivate a blessed soul. By so doing he will display his blessedness by being certain of an everlasting place in heaven.

English novelist, journalist and translator of the Victorian Era, Mary Ann Evans (1819–1880) known by her pen name George Eliot recognized the importance of the influence of a human soul on another when she wrote, "Blessed is the influence on one true, loving human soul on another." American poet, essayist and journalist Walt Whitman (1819–1892) thought, "Whatever satisfies the soul is truth." Undoubtedly, the truth of life will be paramount for the full and authentic development of the soul, which will be set free to enjoy the blessings of the heavenly kingdom.

Thought of the Week

"The Lord redeemeth the soul of His servants: and none of them that trust in Him shall be desolate."

—Psalm 34:22 (KJV)

Meditation 39

Seeds for Souls

It must always be borne in mind that gossip hurts. As you look for guidance from Almighty God, it is best to be obedient to him in life. In everything, pursue wholeness, for it's the basis of enjoyment and good health. An individual that reaches out in doing these things will be blessed with a feeling of worthiness. When helping someone, there should be no strings attached. Do so with an open heart and mind, and let nothing disturb you. Live a life free from fear and embrace its true goodness.

Be always sure of yourself as you live, touch lives, and change lives for the better by being gracious and kind. With such actions, you'll be creating a future of hopefulness. You must depend less on a competitive spirit and more on one that is willing to share and help others. With these natural seeds, bonds will grow through nurturing families, friends, neighbors, and strangers. William Shakespeare (1564–1616), who is regarded as the greatest writer of the English language observed, "It is not in the stars to hold our destiny but in ourselves."

The Earth College

"Our duty is to encourage everyone in his struggle to live up to his own highest ideal, and strive at the same time to make the ideal as near as possible to the Truth." So wrote Indian Hindu monk Swami Vivekananda (1863-1902). Finding truth has to be an ideal in the Earth College.

It's often said that you get what you wish for. Approach life as if you're looking for "your true love" in all things when nurturing diverse talents. Everyone has at least one talent and are all students attending their first Earth College—the college of life. Some of us are handicapped. We may be born that way, but others may be so through ailments that affect them physically, emotionally, and psychologically. Regardless of our status in life—whether able-bodied or handicapped, there are important lessons to learn, and it's best to master them as early as you can. Try your best so that you do not have to repeat them. This is why we ought to share our ideals with those we meet. View all men and women as friends and companions on a life's journey, each distinct in his or her own way.

Live ethically, and do not lie. Honor others and whenever possible give them a helping hand. Be a Good Samaritan to the downtrodden and poor, for remember that we are all students on planet earth. Whatever you achieve do fairly. Do not cheat, nor steal, but work diligently to make a living, and God will surely bless your efforts. Let your ultimate goal be focused on serving and loving others. Be compassionate when illness and suffering come to fellow parishioners, members of your community, and the world. When pursuing what is good, these should be some of your immediate goals.

Love as a Bridge
Ellen G. White (1827–1915), an American author and Christian pioneer of the Seventh-Day Adventist Church felt, "A Christian reveals true humility by showing the gentleness of Christ, by being always ready to help others, by speaking kind words and performing unselfish acts, which elevate and en-noble the most sacred message that has come to the world."

Many times love calls for making baby steps. It's best to take things slowly rather than not doing them at all. This is the cup of hope from which we should all drink. As we live to the fullest, and in pursuit of the good things of life, our personal goals and desires must be based on love. When doing daily chores, our guardian angels are with us as we reach out to people daily. They help us build a bridge to those we love as well as to the unlovable. This truth about life we must not try to resist or deny, for we are to approach others with pure hearts and open minds, while wishing everyone the best for what they are able to do.

In so doing, regardless of our circumstances, we'll be endeavoring to give comfort to those we ought to love. This is a way of freely giving back to the universe. Do remember to be of good cheer and to greet each other with a smile. Take action by extending a helping hand, let people know that you stand with them in their difficulties. "This my friend," is the personal power of love promoting itself like a bridge to every unassuming soul. With every man, woman and child we encounter, love makes a sacred statement. We must never deny loving and caring for others. It's John F. Kennedy (1917–1963), the thirty-fifth president who wisely stated, "As we express our gratitude, we must never forget that the highest appreciation is not to utter words, but to live by them." Our actions are the utmost promises for sowing fertile seeds eternally.

Thought of the Week

"And all the tithe of the land, whether the seed of the land, or the fruit of the tree, is the Lord's: it is holy unto the Lord."

—Leviticus 27:30 (KJV)

Meditation 40

Home of Homes

Our real home is not on earth. It's definitely not in this world in which there's a display of an abundance of dwellings that are of all sizes, styles and shapes. To find one's real home, one needs to be strengthened and enlightened in heavenly ways—to be worthy of true love by our Maker, know the truth and mysteries of faith, and abide by God's authentic commandments. We must learn to forgive and forget wrongs by our friends and enemies alike. Lack of forgiveness robs us from finding our precious gift in heaven.

In attaining spiritual gifts, individuals' paths will be illuminated with clean minds and hearts. One day through the power of prayer, they will be assured of arriving at their true heavenly home. Much of this journey calls for patience and perseverance. It was a Chinese philosopher Confucius (551–497 BC), who taught, "The strength of a nation derives from the integrity of the home." Confucius appears to be speaking about our earthly home, but undoubtedly strength, through our integrity, can only be found in "our home of homes" which is our spiritual home, heaven.

Our Earthly Home

Our earthly homes are wrecked by the horrors of sin—death, disease, malnutrition, poverty and hunger. Many who fight wars do so at their own risk, for these combatants there are spiritual risks. On earth we're bombarded by adversity, contagion and bad examples that constantly spell death. People are led astray by worldly enticements that they may not even realize. What we find therefore is needless suffering as angry nations rise up against each other. These experiences of the pits and bogs of life often call for sacrifices of blood, sweat and tears. As we go about our daily tasks, with impatient minds and hearts, there's a lack of self control, for we live in impatient societies where instant gratification has become the norm. This mediocrity of lifestyle can only lead to the loss of our heavenly home, where we're meant to go and where we must aim for, as our final destination of our earthly sojourn.

Elizabeth Kübler-Ross (1926–2004), a Swiss-American psychiatrist and pioneer in near-death studies observed, "The beautiful people we have known are those who have known defeat, known suffering, known struggle, known loss, and have found their way out of those depths." Despite how dire the world's situation may look, there's always hope for us which was attested to, by Kubler-Ross. We can still find our way out of these perils.

A Willing Spirit

To leave these deadly realities in the world, a believer must constantly spread the spirit of goodness. He or she must be an effective instrument that touches people wherever he or she may go. It calls for taking up his or her cross, bearing its weight squarely on his or her shoulders, and pushing on for the prize. This Christian's mission must be undertaken with a gladness of heart. When you sin you must confess to Almighty God and be certain that you're forgiven and that your life is in order. By so doing, you'll be declaring yourself a new and trusting soul to others, with a clean and steadfast heart. In sustaining a willing spirit and realizing that the truth will set you free, you must let this be your goal. In so doing you'll be honoring the Most High in your ministry. In declaring the power of the Holy Spirit that has performed miracles you'll be praising "a true God and true man," (Hebrews 2:5-18 NRSV), who walked upon the surface of this earth.

Carlos Santana (b. 1947), a Mexican and an American musician observed, "The most valuable possession you can own is an open heart. The most powerful weapon you can be is an instrument of peace." Mahatma Gandhi (1869–1948), a preeminent leader of India's independence movement against the British found, "Power is of two kinds. One is obtained by the fear of punishment and the other by acts of love. Power based on love is a thousand times more effective and permanent than the one derived from fear of punishment." As we walk in this conflicted world, Christians must be armed with the weapons of peace and love.

Our Eternal Home

After lives of faithful service our eternal home will be our gift. It's not the service itself that gets us into paradise, but the grace of God freely given to humankind. Service to believers, is just an outpouring of the spirit made manifest through good acts and deeds. In paradise, believers will be blessed with unending and everlasting joy. With their deliverance, there will be profound happiness and thanksgiving where as angels of true light as opposed to false light - ("And no wonder! Even Satan disguises himself as an angel of light." - 2 Corinthians 11:14 NRSV), will delight in the splendor of holiness. In their blessed goodness, they will be rewarded with everlasting crowns. This is where we'll end up saying, like Rabindranath Tagore (1861–1941), a Bengal artist who reshaped Bengali literature, "I slept and dreamt that life was joy. I woke up and saw that life was service. I acted and behold, service was joy." Come to think about it, this joy will be unimaginable. What glorious blessings awaits us in our home of homes—heaven.

Thought of the Week
"But now they desire a better country, that is, an heavenly: wherefore God is not ashamed to be called their God: for He hath prepared for them a city."

—Hebrews 11:16 (KJV)

Superb Joy

Meditation 41

Joy of Faith

THE JOY OF faith is contagious. Each day it comes like the light of God that shines brighter and brighter. In short, it's our daily bread dished out for us to taste its sweetness. This heavenly delicacy, which accompanies us on our faith journey, is sweeter than honey. Faith is a free and everlasting gift that has no limits. It's special and supernatural to us. Supremely it's like heaven on earth as we tread through its fields picking beautiful flowers. This journey is through the loving care of our Physician of souls who dwells on high. In our Godly orchestrated world, we move independently - each with a special passion, walking by faith, and not by sight. During these moments, peace is revealed in every obedient soul.

Vincent Van Gogh (1853–1890), a major Dutch Post-Impressionist painter with far reaching influence in twentieth-century art professed, "I am still far from being what I want to be, but with God's help I shall succeed." Van Gogh was attesting to God's goodness and guidance in his faith walk. So, why won't we do the same?

Joyful Witness

Let your shout for joy penetrate the night air. Witness happily, by showing an attitude of thanksgiving to our Savior that's loving and just. God became our bread and feeds us with an abundance of blessings. For our benefit, he has bestowed on us the gift of knowledge. As a testament to his many gifts, innovators have invented engines, machines and devices that have made our lives simpler and more enjoyable. Daily, God's sustenance continues to fascinate our souls. We journey from place to place through life with confidence, patience and perseverance. While doing so, we're relentlessly storming heaven with prayers for all good things and benefits of life. Such persistent prayers bring relief to souls that are unable to find life's blessings and satisfaction.

Journey of Faith

An American professor of Internet Law at Harvard School of Engineering and Applied Sciences, Johnathan Zittrain (b. 1969) remarked, "If you entrust your data to others, they can let you down or outright betray you." In modern society which depends on the flow of data, Zittrain's statement is sensible and appropriate. However in the Internet world there are instances of betrayal and much concern about security. But whatever we do, we have to continue to trust others, and have faith that they will do what's in our best interest. Entrusting others is most important for the proper functioning of all sectors of our society. Such a task is never easy but depends on the light of faith, for he's the true bread of life on whom we depend for sustenance. For his gifts, we rejoice in the Creator who provides all things.

Most Christians grow in faith through their church. By the gift of the church, they become better and look forward to the day when they will be blessed with heavenly crowns. Authentic Christians are rich in wisdom and we can see this when they display grace. Their love for the divine is made known to the world. They know their security is abundant when their souls are at peace. Souls that are healed, fruitful and blessed are like shining lights to all men.

A Chinese philosopher, poet and founder of Taoism, Lao Tzu (604–531 BC) observed, "The journey of a thousand miles begins with one step." This expression is faith-filled because accomplishments may not necessary come in the form of mountains or leaps and bounds, but in the form of a little mustard seed that flourishes abundantly.

A Flicker of Light
In John 5:35 (NRSV) stated, "He was a burning and shining lamp, and you were willing to rejoice for awhile in his light." Sometimes all it takes is only a flicker to illuminate a dark pathway. Such is the essence of faith that brings light in our lives. Truly, a spark will enlighten our darkest deeds. This may be demonstrated by how we care and treat God's creation, which a special gift to us.

In modern society we live in the comfort of our homes where we shelter from the elements and enjoy a family life. We must not we forget that once our journey is complete, we look forward to the beauty and prestige of God's heavenly Kingdom. What a joyful day that will be when we must pass through the spiritual gates of acceptance and love. But now we must tend to the welfare of souls who dwell amongst us. Let us delight in the spirit and have a dialogue with souls yearning to be set free to ascend to heavenly places. This is why on every continent each Sunday, Christians flock to churches to be invigorated in their ongoing mission of faith.

Thought of the Week
"If you do not stand firm in faith, you shall not stand at all."

—Isaiah 7:9 (NRSV)

Meditation 42

Heart of Love
Let your heart become one of boundless love. Kindle new love with tenderness and affection. Let your outflow be like that of a fiery furnace

that's perpetually burning. Live a life full of love by reaching out to all—rich and poor alike. Allow those that you love to become the joy of your heart and you'll be like a shining light in the midst of darkness. In our conflicted world you'll be viewed like a flame of hope. It was Joseph Addison (1672–1719), an English playwright and politician who wrote, "Three grand essentials to happiness in this life are something to do, something to love, and something to hope for." So, work for a lasting peace, love all humanity, and hope that all swords will be beaten into plowshares.

Indestructible Love

You must view your love as a pathway to hearts. Capture the true essence of love and clearly follow its way to all goodness. Be triumphant in your quest, embrace and kiss an indescribable love. By so doing, you'll discover the light of joy shining brightly like the sun in a clear blue sky. In short, you'll become one of many lights of the world that saints are. After you'll say like Hosea Ballou (1771–1852), an American Universalist theologian and clergyman, "Tears of joy are like the summer raindrops pierced by sunbeams." Now, you'll be expressing a profound empathy when touched by love, through tears that will be trickling down your cheeks.

Love Beyond Love

Let love beyond love be your battle cry. It's the kind of love that seeks only hearts that will be able to contain it. As it longs for deeper fulfillment, this is complete love that makes the heart burn. In a relationship of love with families, neighbors and friends, reach out to your village, community and town and even to the length and breath of this world. This is when you'll touch the ecstasy of love that brings true joy and peace. Such is complete joy that an individual can only find in Jesus Christ. It's a profound joy of hope and faith. Moreover, this joy when it's engulfed by the light of all light, will herald hope that touches souls. French soldier, military theorist and commander during World War I Ferdinand Foch (1851–1929) declared, "The most powerful weapon on earth is the human soul on fire."

Power of Love

Love is a dynamic force. Initially, it begins by warming the heart and eventually makes it purely joyful. This gladness is replete with respect for the diversity of the human race. Its fundamental tenets can be found in the Gospel of the Lord. Through the light of faith readers of these works are able to view what it means to live in the spirit in a new way. Many will be touched by the light of faith and readers of scripture will be able to see themselves in newer ways. Bengali literary figure Rabindranath Tagore (1861–1941) explained, "Faith is the bird that feels the light when dawn is still dark."

The power of love stirs our imagination and guides us to do the impossible. It reaches out to our animate and inanimate worlds turning them into true bliss. With love all good things and even human suffering raise our consciousness to an elevated plane, where mortals will one day become immortal. It was Jesus Christ the creator of this reality, who demonstrated this. His sacrifice, death, resurrection and ascension were glorious. Showing his power of supernatural love was so remarkable that it has become the foundational stone for mankind. Jesus was the stone that the builders rejected yet was made the cornerstone of our hope.

It took this humble act, submission and godly perfection to accomplish an extraordinary feat. It was only through grace that we can begin to understand and appreciate his action. Christ is the epitome of the power of love. His was a clarion call to believers and unbelievers alike, to realize this. Initially, there were many doubters concerning His saving grace. Even one of his own disciples—Thomas—had to touch his wounds to believe. It's clear however, that those of faith will be able to express this superb love by their belief. "Love conquers all." All faith-propelled love, is the catalyst of supreme love.

Thought of the Week

"But the Lord said to Samuel, 'Do not look on his appearance or on the height of his stature, because I have rejected him; for the Lord does not see as mortals see, they look on the outward appearance, but the Lord looks on the heart.'"

—1 Samuel 16:7 (NRSV)

Meditation 43

Blessed Joy

Seek a blessed joy that illuminates your path to happiness and let it vivify your spirit with ecstasy. Necessary though, is having a contrite heart, clean mind and generous spirit. This is the basis of having such a perfect gift from the Almighty. You'll be the truest of lights that's ideal in your Christian walk of patience and perseverance. Barack Obama (b. 1961), the forty-fourth president of the United States and first African American to hold this office said, "If you're walking down the right path and you're willing to keep walking, eventually you will make progress." Undoubtedly, a faith-walk will lead to bliss and an enlightened heart.

Not the Joy of the World

The joys of this world are fleeting. In the right way worldly joy does not adapt and adjust. True joy is the weapon of the spirit, defeating the terror of men that are troubled and distressed by their deeds. In the world, there's filth, sin, and a fear of the future. In the eyes of a Christian, his or her future is always bright. He or she lives according to the promises of God and is faithful and kind to mankind. Nevertheless, like all worldly sinners, he or she faces temporary hardships that are like pinpricks as compared to the glorious life that awaits him or her in heaven.

Our world is confronted with an array of hardships. If it's not war, murder, poverty, or crime, much of it is sensual pleasure. Many people hold their heads high, walk with their chests up and are puffed up. At its best, this is a display of vanity. Time and time again as people confront great struggles, they suffer broken hearts but continue to pretend that everything is fine. It must be remembered that we can't depend on the things of this world for true comfort. We hear and see in the media empty praise and double talk with some groveling on earth. As though bound in fetters, worldly types live by the wind of fickleness. An American poet, essayist and philosopher Ralph Waldo Emerson (1803–1882) observed, "To be yourself in a world that is constantly trying to make you something else is the greatest accomplishment." To be true to oneself, must be the aim of every Christian who lives in troubled places of this world.

Spreading Joy

It's right and just that a Christian go about his or her life spreading joy and hope. To be a true Christian is to live joyfully. Being sustained by the Holy Spirit evangelize and minister constantly. As a light of the world, and with humble heart, walk confidently as a peace maker in the midst of wolves. In embracing the ecstasy of your heart and mind, love faithfulness, fly freely and with an elevated spirit, and teach and proclaim the truth of all things seen and unseen. Such a walk will be completely filled with riches of the heavenly kingdom. Robert H. Schuller (1926–2015), an American Christian televangelist, pastor, and motivational speaker testified to such a walk when he stated, "God flourished my ministry and my career of creative thinking, communicating and writing back fifty years." Over so many years it was Schuller's belief that our Lord and Savior, Jesus Christ blessed his life's mission abundantly in distinct ways.

Comforting Joy

In the Gospel for comforting joy, it's best to review Jesus, his disciples and his apostles' teachings. Their testimonies and wisdom are like stars that mirror the bright lights of the Christian life. By having a shield of faith, be steadfast in your understanding of the Word. It must be remembered that on the day of judgment, we'll have to account for the lives we have lived. It's comforting to know that Christians of true faith can look forward to the heavenly consolation. All their sins will be washed away, and they will be whiter than snow. In our hearts, this is the spiritual fervor and belief that we must hold dearly. To be comforted daily with blessedness, a pure heart and clean mind are the beginnings of a true faith-walk. Strengthened inwardly, it'll then be right to claim that we'll have ascended to sublime heights by the love of our Lord and Savior, Jesus Christ.

It was Ann Landers (1918–2002), a *Chicago Sun-Times* advice columnist, who reminded us to, "expect trouble as an inevitable part of life and repeat to yourself; the most comforting words of all; this, too, shall pass." For Christians, this realization is inevitable - for they also know the victory has already been won, and supreme greatness awaits them in heaven.

Thought of the Week
"Restore to me the joy of your salvation, and sustain in me a willing spirit."

—Psalm 51:12 (NRSV)

Meditation 44

Inspiration of Hope
Without hope, there's no fullness of life. Hope makes a broken world a more habitable place. It enlivens the church with extraordinary faith, for Christ lives at the center of its experience. Christians are therefore blessed with hope-filled minds and offer hope to the world. To believers, hope is like faith. Much of this faith is gained in living by the dogged pursuit of the Gospel of Our Lord and Savior, Jesus Christ. Once converted, a believer is caught up in the Holy Spirit and is blessed by the heavenly physician of souls. These blessings are celebrated by the faithful participation in the Eucharistic rite.

One of the most productive of his time, an American inventor Thomas Edison (1847–1931) remarked, "Genius is one percent inspiration, ninety-nine percent perspiration." It was obvious that Edison thought that we must be dogged about our commitments to obtain the best results. This is why a little inspiration like a mustard seed, is enough for great motivation and achievements.

A Renewed Human Spirit

Initiating love and being loved are excellent virtues. With all the beloved, love drives fervent hope. It's changing but doesn't hope. We'll never want to be deprived of the hope of living in Christ. It's the everlasting flame that is sound, good and just. Be inspired by hope, live righteously and reach out to the world around you. With an air of respectability, put on the cloak of patience and perseverance, for a heavenly consolation awaits you. With every deed, be the symbol of heavenly grace in your community by blessing the earth with your presence. Hunger for the heavenly gifts just and right. Pray daily storming the gates of heaven in seeking God's freedom.

It was Francis Bacon (1561–1626), an English philosopher and statesman who observed, "The inquiry of truth, which is love-making, or the wooing of it, the knowledge of truth, which is the presence of it, and the belief of truth, which is the enjoying of it, is the sovereign good of human nature." This is in the steadfast hope of a sovereign God that brings us to the blessedness of gracious truth which becomes the living and active hope for our souls.

Light of the Lord

You ought to be concerned especially for young children who are the innocent ones of the world. Use hope as one of your godly weapons to trust God for their welfare. Always remember that issues that affect the weak are global in dimension. To be truly blessed, calls for our great Christian hope to be steadfast in every enterprise we undertake in God's name. With fruits of patience, we labor in the trenches to promote goodness in and for man. These actions often call for patience and courage because there will always be evil forces that will endeavor to hinder our work. It's impossible to control evil although we can counter it with God's help. When we do, we're expressing love and casting our eyes toward the gifts of the kingdom of heaven not the kingdom of man.

Then we can declare like Charles Wesley (1701–1788), an English Methodist hymn-writer and brother of John Wesley:

"Jesu, thou art all compassion,
Pure unbounded love thou art;
Visit us with thy salvation,
Enter every trembling heart."

Be a Force against Principalities and Powers

God's hope is a force against principalities and powers. We know that the rulers of darkness can never have true hope. They are robbed of their hope because of their devious behavior and actions. Believers must therefore bear patiently with their onslaughts and bring them before God who alone knows the hearts of all men. Be rich in heavenly wisdom. By proclaiming the truth you oppose errors in judgment, and challenge desperate acts of unrighteousness. Your experience will make you bask in the glimmerings of the glory of heaven even as you live on planet earth. Believers are assured that the wicked will have no place in heaven.

Edmund Burke (1729–1797), an Anglo-Irish statesman who became the secretary of Ireland observed, "The use of force is but temporary. It may subdue for a moment, but it does not remove the necessity of subduing again..." This temporary force is what tyrants put their trust in. But true Christian hope is marked by everlasting joy, peace and goodness. Be inspired by the hope of God that will be the salvation to all believers.

Thought of the Week

"And now faith, hope, and love abide, these three; and the greatest of these is love."

—1 Corinthians 13:13 (NRSV)

Meditation 45

Joy of Serenity

The joy of serenity is a quiet joy that lights up the soul. It's the tenderness found in love and is infinite goodness. A person with such joy has an open heart, for he or she is willing to accept and forgive everybody. The heart is illuminated and what is born in one's heart is tranquility. Such joy can be found in a believer. A Christian is known to have a spiritual heart of kindness and goodness.

American theologian, ethicist and professor at the Union Theological Seminary in New York Reinhold Niebuhr (1892–1971) prayed, "God grant me the serenity to accept the things I cannot change, the courage to change the things I can, and the wisdom to know the difference." This popular prayer shows insight into a heart that is supreme, and pours out its shortcomings to God to be able to discern was is true, wise and best.

Joyful Experience

Persons of faith light up with joy when they encounter the poor. This is true love that expresses itself in acts of helpfulness. Much fruitful love is manifested from the depths of the heart. It's through the love of service that an individual can touch this reality. Such is the love of Christ taking root in the lives of the repentant. This is love beyond love—one who cares and has passion for the underdog. Now, a Christian concentrates on uplifting the ostracized from their plight of degradation. Such service is considered one of the highest forms of good that is explained in the Gospel of life. It's the face of truth expressing itself freely without inhibitions in our society and can be found in hearts dedicated to the benevolence of mankind. Cleansed hearts truly reveal the joy of well-lived lives.

Eleanor Roosevelt (1884–1962), the first lady of the United States from (1933 to 1945), a politician and diplomat observed, "People grow through experience if they meet life honestly and courageously. This is how character is built." This is true of all Christians with serene hearts who are willing to serve. Their actions build character and impact those they encounter in their lifetime.

The Wine of Joy

Wine is a festive drink. Through it joy is born, and there are many associations and much symbolism that describe its remarkable presence. It can be best described as the service of love that flows at weddings, that is poured out during the Eucharistic feast and that is used for medicinal purposes. With wine there's mystery all by itself. Hearts are known to burn with its essence, which generates joy by telling the good news of Christ and his spirit of truth. Wine at Mass becomes a lightning rod that peps up holiness in a church's gathering. It pierces the fabric of hearts, making them one community. Like old wine, it's the ideal catalyst in our midst that changes hearts which signifies the heart of humanity.

Pope John XXIII (1881–1963), who presided from October 28, 1958, until his death in 1963 and was canonized on April 27, 2014 summarized the effect of wine on men best, "Men are like wine—some turn to vinegar, but the best improve with age." Improvement yes! The desire to better ourselves, as we continue our journey through life, must always be foremost on our minds. It must be the purpose of our quest, as we endeavor to live purpose-driven lives.

Joy of Peace

The thirty-sixth president of the United States Lyndon B. Johnson (1908–1973) said, "Peace is a journey of a thousand miles and it must be taken one step at a time."

Oh, light eternal, the maker of peace, let us shine our lights of peace to all mankind. Like with president Johnson's notion, these lights will be steadfast, never letting our batteries run low, for the distance is great. This is the expression of genuine love, and concern to all men—rich, poor and indifferent alike—especially those who are our enemies. We can capture such serenity through the dialogue of love, care and steadfastness. This is boundless, and it transcends all things that express themselves in the goodness of creation. It's why we must not be afraid of practicing goodness, which some may consider a weakness. Our focus must be on the Good Shepherd, who is the purveyor of peace and tranquility. We know that we have achieved our ultimate goal of peace with our neighbor and enemy, when we come away with peace engraved in our hearts and serene minds.

Thought of the Week

"...from whom the whole body, joined and knit together by every ligament with which it is equipped, as each part is working properly, promotes the body's growth in building itself up in love."

—Ephesians 4:16 (NRSV)

Meditation 46

Joy of Our Hearts

The joy of our hearts causes joyful proclamations. This is when the heart shines brightly with the love of light. To achieve this state takes patience and perseverance. A Christian yearns for such bliss. With fervent hope there must be a goal set to arrive at this place in one's journey of life. Much of this is attained by viewing the world as a support system for the common good of humankind. Being good, just and holy are exemplary of the happiness with which a person is engulfed. Such a Christian has a passion for social justice and champions the rights of the underprivileged. A wind of Pentecost greets such a reformer. He isn't necessarily an evangelist-in-chief, but a humble devotee to the faith of Christ.

Joseph Conrad (1857–1924), a Polish born British novelist observed, "I remember my youth and the feeling that it will never come back any more—the feeling that I could last forever, outlast the sea, the earth and all men; the deceitful feeling that lures us on to joys, to perils, to love, to vain effort—to death, the triumphant conviction of strength, the heart of life in the handful of dust, the glow in the heart...." This captures brilliantly the life of youth, with reflections of what it meant to Conrad. This quote shows a young heart venting to deep feelings.

Joy Changes

Momentarily, there are temporal joys. Folks may experience hills of unexpected peaks mixed with unexpected undulating valleys. It may take patience to weave an elusive feeling of a heart of joy. This is a flame of hope that must try to embrace and sustain us. To accomplish this calls for an encounter with the truth of beauty itself. There's nothing more trustworthy in achieving this than by reading and studying the Word of Truth. Through it, the teachings of the Good Shepherd will come alive in its brilliance. You'll need to pursue this mission faithfully. This is an effort that calls for being a witness of the Christian faith. Argentinian poet and novelist Ricardo Güiraldes (1886–1927) remarked, "If you are really a gaucho, you can't change, because wherever you go, you'll go with your soul leading the way." Much of what a person becomes is based on what he or she has been throughout his life. That's why as joy changes our underlying nature, it will reveal our true selves.

Purity of Heart

A pure heart will best express joy. Concentrating on the fruits of patience will bring about changes in the deepest recesses of our being. This calls for courage in a believer's heart. The great Christian hope of peacefulness awaits a seeker of this precious gift. With the goal of securing the highest good an individual will walk confidently in faith. A person must not be afraid of goodness nor view it like some in the world do—as some sort of weakness. The fullest truth is expressed by the Holy Spirit. To accomplish this task, every Christian must view him- or herself as an athlete for Christ. During the course of his or her lifetime he or she must be prepared to run many marathons. His or her faith is in encountering Jesus Christ, for he or she will be rubbing shoulders and touching the flesh of Christ through the poor and hungry that he or she meets.

Matthew 22:37 (KJV) quoted Jesus as saying, "Thou shalt love the Lord thy God with all thy heart, and with all thy soul, and with all thy mind." Christ's love, at its purest is encompassing.

Angels of Light

Those with a joyful heart are undoubtedly lights in the world, because their hearts are in the right place. A person must never lose hope concerning this truth. He must think about justice and hopefulness and everything will fall into place. This is the foundation of abundant goodness best expressed in the creation which we enjoy. Christians mainly do so by adoring the beauty of God himself. In all divinity, he's the true incarnation that's glorified. Reading and contemplating the seeds of the Gospel are like an eye-opener to a believer. Through prayer and meditation and with the ticktock of consciousness, seeds of hopefulness are spread around the world, even if it isn't windy. This is only done by the flame of faith that's the joy of our heart.

Robert Burns (1759–1796), a Scottish writer and one of the world's most popular poets wrote:

"The golden Hours, on angel wings
Flew o'er me and my Dearie;
Was my sweet 'Highland Mary.'"

A true angel of light represents the best in life. "Highland Mary' may well be likened to Holy Mary, Mother of God, and her faith, which is the joy of our hearts.

Thought of the Week

"...the fear of the Lord is pure, enduring forever; the ordinances of the Lord are true and righteous altogether."

—Psalm 19:9 (NRSV)

Meditation 47

Ecstasy of Joy

Experiencing the ecstasy of joy is an extraordinary blessing. This is when a Christian recognizes that he or she has ascended to the mountain top of life. Filled with joy such a person is on top of the world looking down at its valleys below. Light engulfs his or her being and he or she is enlightened by the glory of his overview. A few saints who have attained such a state were known for their humility. At times they have also experienced great despair. Now these are holy, heavenly endowed lights who are honored by the heavenly physician of souls who has mysteriously guided them to this point. Having an everlasting soul has assured them and they'll be in an exalted state for eternity. This is the great secret of a happy life that's the most important lesson Christians are taught.

It's said in the *De Dignitate et Augmentis Scientiarum, Antitheta* no. 9 (1623) translated by Gilbert Watts in 1640, "The voice of the people hath some divineness in it, else how should so many men agree to be on one mind?" Such a mindset is what a Christian will accomplish in an exalted state. There will be hills and valleys, but rest assured, there will also be ecstatic joy—the highest form of delight.

Joy of Freshness

There are some persons who will want to do anything possible to accomplish this kind of joy. At best it's sacrificial as demonstrated by our greatest teacher, Jesus Christ. Some saints have suffered martyrdom and been greatly honored in their lives. They have been assured of receiving heavenly crowns of martyrdom for everlasting life. They have embraced life's hardships in precious ways. Through their actions and bathed in divine light, souls were healed and brought to the light. Most apparent is the beauty of love during their sacrifices for Christ. Throughout the ages, such sacrificial love has formed a bridge of love to all Christians. That's why at churches we hear priests preach about the great deeds of the saints. With compassionate living we're called to embrace hardships by following the Lord's example on the cross.

Living a life in the footsteps of Jesus is the most delightful thing that a Christian can do. It's best for us to be preachers by the way we live in the world, for it must be remembered that a Christian's goal must be to transform lives. There's supreme joy in heaven when one lost soul is won and set on the right path of life. This is the joy and dignity in discovering a Christian lifestyle.

A credo engraved in Rockefeller Center Plaza, New York reveals, "The rendering of useful service is the common duty of mankind, and…only the purifying fire of sacrifice is the dress of selfishness consumed and the greatness of the human soul set free." What an inspiration this is for yearning souls waiting to be set free to be all they can be!

Mother of Joy

Ecstasy is the mother of joy. It brings true gladness to the heart, mind and soul, radiating light that touches all men who are seeking divine goodness, by being lights of love of the church. In this path, there's always an abiding truth that has endowed our spirit in living to the fullest. At best it's the epitome for truth found in loving our Lord and Savior Jesus Christ. His notion propels us to embrace the everlasting way.

In Sonnet 33, William Shakespeare (1564–1616), of England wrote:

"Full many a glorious morning have I seen
Flatter the mountain tops with sovereign eye,
Kissing with golden face the meadows green."

With these beautiful lines, Shakespeare has surely captured the absolute mountain-top joy of nature. It's truly superb and full of light, refreshing the soul that sparks the Christian mission to take care of the wonderful blessings of our earthly paradise. This great love expresses itself for the protection of the environment that God has so graciously created. The power of love is a genuine expression for caretakers of nature's bounty. It's joy that has to be shown and nurtured in the deepest possible way—by how we live and relate to nature.

We can find such encouragement in the Word. Within its pages we're able to taste the excellent possibilities that are ours to have. Here we can look forward to the greatest blessing of all—everlasting life, where we'll be living to the fullest extent in a life of splendor for all eternity.

Thought of the Week

"And if children, then heirs; heirs of God, and joint-heirs with Christ; if so be that we suffer with Him, that we may be glorified together."

—Romans 8:17 (KJV)

Team Spirit

Meditation 48

By Special Authority

YOU'RE A LEADER and by your special God-given authority, you have to energize your entire organization. This means finding ways to deal with assignments that appear as though they don't have a chance of working. It's up to you to diagnose their problems. Your responsibility must not be seen as a power play, for you're working for the welfare of the church. It's always good to remember that you're not carrying out a private agenda, but are working for the goodwill of all concerned. It was Vince Lombardi (1913–1970), an American football player, best known as the head coach of the Green Bay Packers— who wrote, "The achievements of an organization are the results of the combined effort of each individual." Thus you'll have to realize each church member is gifted and it's through their gifts that there will be eventual success. This is why you have to pull together to do what is best for your community.

Maximize Potential

People ought to be treated like adults. Listen to every member and hear what they all have to say. Not everything will work out, but you'll always have another point of view. You must motivate your workers to be happy about what they're doing, and urge them on to higher and higher levels of performance. This is why it's essential to keep tabs on the pulse of the group. In this way you'll know each worker, his or her values, and his or her mode of behavior.

In so doing, you'll be best able to promote the church's growth along with worker competence. Accomplishing these things mean that you'll have to take things a step at a time as you build on each success.

Margaret Mead (1901–1978), an American cultural anthropologist observed, "Never doubt that a small group of thoughtful, committed citizens can change the world; indeed, it's the only thing that ever has." A committed leader will bring his or her followers to this envious state when he or she works on implementing what's best for a congregation and the world at large.

Lack of Authoritarian Control

A leader ought to be people-oriented. In the church, there's no room for tyrants, bullies nor autocrats. With tyrants organizations eventually die. It's the kiss of death even to a well-intentioned and benevolent leader who leads by whim. Let a leader do away with being ego centric, but may he or she be democratic and work in the best interest of the flock. It was "Dr. Seuss"– Theodor Seuss Geisel (1904–1991), an American writer and cartoonist, widely known for his children books who warned, "Only you can control your future." A spirit-filled leader will always lead in the best interest of his flock.

Be an Inspiration

Your role is to help people. To do so effectively you'll have to take ample note of relationships within the church. You have to lead by example and change outmoded methods that no longer work. You must stimulate achievements by expressing your sincere belief in humanity. It's important for parishioners must feel your apostolic zeal. Through the Holy Spirit, and by living life on a higher plane, you'll shy away from the narrowness of self-absorption. In this way, you'll motivate others for the general good.

Lee Haney (b. 1959), an American former professional bodybuilder thought about such inspiration when he reasoned, "Exercise to stimulate, not to annihilate. The world wasn't formed in a day, and neither were we. Set small goals and build upon them." Haney's message is encouraging. Many may be looking for giant steps to be considered successful, but it's always wise to remember that success often comes in small doses. Your goal as a leader is to build on those little achievements until they grow, placing your organization where you wish it to be. So, the lesson you must keep in mind is, "Keep striving and persevere even when the going is rough. For, at the end of every dark cloud, there's a silver lining," is what some people say.

Thought of the Week
"And the spirits of prophets are subject to the prophets, for God is a God not of disorder but peace."

—Corinthians 14:32–33 (NRSV)

Meditation 49

Gifts of the Spirit
It's amazing to be blessed by the gifts of the spirit. Glossolalia, or speaking in tongues, is well known and respected in some Christian churches. Some view these occurrences as the wind of God giving utterance in His people. It can be considered as a dimension of the breath of life. However, such a gift has to be put into its proper perspective. Some Christians may be carried away, and view their utterances like having a mountaintop power of righteousness. However it must be remembered that the various fruits of God are all centered in a life of the spirit. These gifts can be ecstatic, emotional, an illumination, moral, transforming, charismatic, miracles, healing or include a religious awakening.

Ayrton Senna (1960–1994), a Brazilian racing driver who won three Formula One world championships observed, "Wealthy men can't live in an island that is encircled by poverty. We all breathe the same air. We must give a chance to everyone, at least a basic chance." All gifts come from the same source and are like the air we breathe. We must never fall into the trap of making distinctions concerning which gifts are superior, but must promote what's good in the church.

Inspired Prophetic Utterances

All gifts come through the spirit of God. Prophetic utterances may be in the form of speech or writings. We know these authentic works because they are filled with a biblical spirit of enlightenment. The goal of each gift is the same. It's meant to proclaim the risen Christ, his power and resurrection. These works are known for their insights and spiritual depth. They always will proclaim Christ as the center of all things. Christian devotees of these utterances live a life that's steeped in prayer.

We can tell who these Christians are, for, it was a Chinese philosopher Confucius (551–479 BC) who wrote, "The superior man is modest in his speech, but exceeds in his actions." There's the old saying that goes, "Actions speak louder than words." Thus, "Show me how a person lives and you'll be sure about the fruits he bears." If an individual is a faithful Christian, you can very well expect him or her to be active in various ministries in his or her church. More likely that not, he or she will attend church regularly and will be drawn to fellowship with other parishioners.

Agent of Salvation

A true agent is always guided by the Holy Spirit. In his or her walk he or she is impacting, shaping and transforming lives in everyday places. He or she is able to do these things because he or she was baptized in the Holy Spirit, has the power of discernment and sees him- or herself as a full-time missionary. Such a believer is prudent and gifted with the wisdom to know what's right or wrong.

It doesn't stop here. How's he or she free? Ramakrishna (1836–1886), an Indian mystic and yogi during the nineteenth-century proposed, "A man is truly free, even here in his embodied state, if he knows that God is the true agent and he by himself is powerless to do anything." Man's freedom and power are only manifested through his creator.

Believers' Inheritance

A true believer is blessed with sacred hope. His or her service and help are gifts from a loving God. He or she may be in counseling and administration in the church, but through his or her stewardship he or she is able to give aid and mercy to others. A true believer knows that in his or her duties, he or she is propelled by a spirit of benevolence. His or her actions include witnessing and praying. In his or her arsenal, these are the most powerful Christian weapons. Many observers know that he or she is a spiritual force, for he or she is animated by the Holy Spirit, through whom he's accomplishing and will continue to accomplish heavenly goals.

It was Donald Miller (b. 1971), a best-selling American author who focuses on Christian spirituality, who captured this reality best when he argued, "Sunday morning church service is not an enormous priority; spending time with other believers is." The lesson that can be taken away from Miller's statement is that Christian outreach is more than being in the church, but on the highways and byways of life where they are also believers.

Thought of the Week

"Jesus answered and said unto her, If thou knowest the gift of God, and who it is that saith to thee, Give Me to drink; thou wouldest have asked of Him, and He would have given thee living water."

—John 4:10 (KJV)

Meditation 50

Power of the Spirit

With most Christians the power of the Spirit is prominent. They fellowship in the Spirit and act according to divine commands from Almighty God. They hold the scripture to be authoritative. Since Pentecost they have been continually blessed with the outpouring of the Holy Spirit. By this awareness comes overwhelming experiences which are at times accompanied by heavenly visions. As they live according to the life-giving spirit, their utterances are inspired. Being led by the spirit, they walk in the light and are full of life and vitality.

Alexander Pope (1688–1744), an eighteenth-century English poet, best known for his satirical verse, made this famous statement: "To err is human; to forgive, divine." It must never be thought that those who walk in the spirit are not quick to forgive. Like Pope, they do realize that life entails forgiveness for which there are divine and sacred blessings.

Community Spirit

The power of the spirit brings about unifying bonds. These correlate with the interactions of believers with other persons during their lives. These relationships are elevated to the level of divinity and sealed with a bond of friendship. Some followers of the way, marry and form lasting bonds with their spouse. But as members of the church, they may also devote themselves to pastoral outreach. They will come to exemplify what's ideal between the liturgical center and the periphery of worshipers. There will be a natural osmosis between the church's hierarchy and its parishioners.

In the life of the church much thought goes into the role of the sacraments. Every attempt is encouraged to enhance a family's life. Young people are therefore exposed to godly standards concerning what it means to date and be happily married. Christians values are perpetuated as the foundation on which to build relationships inside and outside the church's community.

The Messianic Age

The power of the spirit has ushered in the Messianic Age. It brings hope in its wake by the inspiration of the Gospel. It's the new age of blessings that are bestowed on every believer. Because we're a new creation in Christ, we're inspired by the spirit. This spirit is the one we experience fully in our daily walk. By our industriousness the church will benefit from our talents. Most believers will experience the outpouring of faithfulness that is now a reality through these lights in their midst. It isn't unusual to hear Christians describe with hopeful joy that it feels like heaven on earth.

George Bernard Shaw (1856–1950), an English playwright and co-founder of the London School of Economics observed, "Imagination is the beginning of creation. You imagine what you desire, you will what you imagine and at last create what you will." The Messianic Age is much more than our imagination. It's a superb gift that has been freely given to every man, woman and child, concerning how they must open their hearts to the Lord.

Harvest of Men

Our salvation is guaranteed. It's what God completed on the cross. This state is the seed of divine life open to all who will seek and find Him. It starts with the circumcision of the heart, frees us from legalisms, and it's a gift of charity. While we live, we'll have renewed encounters with the risen Christ. As holy people, we'll be defending the traditions of fidelity in a broken world. Moreover, as baptized Christians we'll be the natural followers of Christ.

Og Mandino (1923-1996), an American author who wrote the best-selling book *The Greatest Salesman in the World* encouraged us to, "Always do your best. What you plant now, you will harvest later." Be sure to sow good seed, for it's promised your harvest will be plentiful. Or, be fishers of men for the Lord, because you're assured your catch will be abundant.

Thought of the Week

"Who shall change our vile body, that it may be fashioned like unto His glorious body, according to the working whereby He is able even to subdue all things unto Himself."

—Philippians 3:21 (KJV)

Meditation 51

Spirit of Fraternity

It must be a Christian's goal to be part of the sisterhood and brotherhood of the spirit of fraternity. Because of this, it's imperative to capture the biblical spirit of our age. We walk in the presence of the Lord and proclaim His omnipotence. In so doing, every Christian will express his or her faith. This authentic fraternity is at its best an unconditional surrender of oneself to God. With such an experience a believer will be tending the afflictions of the wounded among us. Alan Cohen (b. 1939), an American author of inspirational books observed, "Appreciation is the highest form of prayer, for it acknowledged the presence of good wherever you shine the light of thankful thoughts." Undoubtedly, through this fraternity, you'll be shining your light before and on those you meet.

Never Tire of Forgiving

Forgiveness is the basis of a sociable fraternity. Having true friends means that there will be times when you both won't see eye to eye. During these disagreements, it's imperative to reach out to make things right. This will be your way of expressing your freedom of goodness that has manifested itself in you. It's exemplary when you forge bonds that'll endure the test of time. Much of this aspect of your personality may not come easily, but will call for prudence and discernment.

In churches for example - when there are many pastoral challenges and as parishioners practice outreach, there will be disagreements. But the holy people of God should be able to discuss and solve conflicts amicably. As a child of God, let Christian values guide your decisions for the betterment and well-being of all concerned. When Christians do acts of kindness, we are vivified by the spirit. Service itself can be spiritual food that leads to an enlightened community. An enlightened congregation brings an abundance of blessings. It's only through experiences with the working of the Holy Spirit that we're blessed. This is why in relationships of every kind, friendship and fellowship are important.

Charles R. Swindoll (b. 1934), an evangelical Christian pastor, author and radio preacher remarked, "I cannot even imagine where I would be today were it not for that handful of friends who have given me a heart full of joy. Let's face it; friends make life a lot more fun."

Love God and Neighbor

A fraternity of the spirit must be considered a fraternity for the journey. This trip will turn arid land into a garden of roses and express a profound love. Love is courageous and seeks peace in unusual places. This is the depth of love found not only between friends, but with one's enemies as well, and it's best expressed in an all encompassing God —our Lord and Savior Jesus Christ who died for us on the cross at Calvary. With love comes loving-kindness when we embrace each other, but, love has to be constantly sown and cultivated to reap an abundant harvest. Leo Buscaglia (1924–1998), an American author and motivational speaker taught that "a single rose can be my garden…a single friend, my world." Our abundance in the world may well be one person. Such a blessing is qualitative and not quantitative.

Be Animated by the Spirit

The focus of the spirit of fraternity is that of the risen Christ. Believers who are members of his club are animated by his spirit. It's a spirit of fervor that manifests itself within us. Christ is a true comforter, providing us with spiritual food when needed, and seeing Christians motivated by their Apostolic zeal. For thousands of years, since the outpouring of the spirit on the feast of Pentecost, this occasion has been a tremendous blessing to every Christian. Our spiritual journey is continually deepened by innumerable spiritual experiences. Some in the brotherhood and sisterhood fraternity are known for their steadfast spirit of love, joy, hope and peace.

Every believer must make it essential for spreading the spirit. As for our devout fraternity, it's God who anoints those who are trustworthy. It's God who empowers us to do great works for him on earth. A fraternity's walk is by faith and not by sight for they are all truly blessed.

Thought of the Week
"Thou shalt not bear false witness against thy neighbor."

—Exodus 20:16 (KJV)

Meditation 52

Team of Works
When working with others it serves us well to cultivate a team spirit. This may be in a church, an organization, a corporation or a sport. It's worthy to note that a team spirit begins by treating others with respect. It's true that there are different positions at your job, but all workers must be made to feel that their job is important, and for the common good of their company. There will be defined goals depending on the nature of your work. If you happen to be in the field of journalism, the goal may be to stay objective" when seeking the truth of a story. Before making decisions within the church, parishioners often pray for guidance by the Holy Spirit. These are the beginnings of ethical leadership.

An English cricket commentator John Arlott (1914–1991) observed, "Cricket is a game of the most terrifying stresses with more luck about it than any other game I know. They will call it a team game, but in fact it is the loneliest game of all." What Arlott noted is true about cricket, but as with other responsibilities of any job, there's still the individual whose role it is to coordinate such activities. On occasion, a team member will be isolated, and he or she often has to make independent decisions. These have to be for the good of the team.

Workers Must Listen to Their Conscience
Call it conscience, the Holy Spirit or God—workers must listen to that small voice that speaks in secret to them. They must be conscious of their values. Good values are compatible with the teachings of the scriptures. Obtaining

scriptural assurances or confirmation through a trusted colleague who will signal that you're on the right track is advantageous. A worker must listen carefully to instructions, be slow to speak and always remember that he or she is important in partnership with fellow workers. In church he or she must take direction from the Evangelizer-in-Chief – the priest or the Holy Spirit— before doing a task. Before taking a leap often a prayer to the Almighty will suffice. At all times people must have their finger on the pulse of the work place to see if their directions coincide with the main mission. This is especially true when a leader's exercising a special kind of authority with followers.

Edmund Burke (1729–1797), an Anglo-Irish statesman and political philosopher said, "Society is indeed a contract...it becomes a partnership not only between those that are living, those who are dead, and those who are to be born." Burke has definitely touched on the fact that we're interrelated – physically, intellectually, emotionally and spiritually. Although these relationships may be beyond our present awareness and comprehension, they are about humanity, and are meant to be for our work's growth and development.

Influence in Church

Believers must be spiritually enabled. Their aim must be the achievement of a high standard of spiritual growth in their church. Many times such responsibility falls on the parish priest who demonstrates this leadership. But all adult members of the congregation ought to be groomed to shoulder this shared responsibility—a partnership based of the teachings of the Gospel. Whenever there's the decision on a liturgical matter, the parish members must give their input. When undertaking projects, the leaders of the parish committees will have to be sure that they are exercising legitimate power. This is when they will know how to accept wise counsel for the benefit of all parishioners. This process will inevitably be one way leaders can enhance their status in the community.

Wassily Kandinsky (1866–1944), a Russian born painter and writer, stated, "The force that propels the human spirit on the clear way forward and upward is the abstract spirit." That's why within the church, it's wise to pray prior to making decisions when setting a project in motion. Keep praying throughout the entire process, for it's the Holy Spirit who sanctions and enlivens our work.

Spirit of Enthusiasm
An American philosopher, poet and a central figure of the transcendentalist movement Ralph Waldo Emerson (1803–1882) remarked, "Nothing great was ever achieved without enthusiasm." Jesus's disciples were a handful of rough and generally unlearned men, but they were gifted with a driving power to get the job done. Many Christians have come to be blessed by the comforting joy of evangelizing. It is remarkable how such a team spirit is gradually built. Mainly, their task is undertaken often by faith and their belief in the project. Because it takes team spirit to minister effectively, this comes down to sharing our dreams with the Lord. With some believers there will be debate and conflict, but their enthusiasm will be driven by doing what's best for the church.

Thought of the Week
"Blessed are ye, when men shall revile you, and persecute you, and shall say all manner of evil against you falsely, for My sake.

Rejoice, and be exceedingly glad: for great is your reward in heaven..."

—Matthew 5:11–12 (KJV)

Selected Readings

à Kempis, Thomas. 2003. *The Imitation of Christ*. Translated by Aloysius Croft and Harold Bolton. Mineola, NY: Dover Publications, Inc.

Barnhill, Carla, ed. 2005. *A Year with Dietrich Bonhoeffer*. New York: HarperCollins Publishers.

Bennett, William J. 1993. *The Book of Virtues*. New York: Simon & Schuster.

Birch, David, ed. 2015. *The Wisdom of Pope Francis*. New York: Skyhorse Publishing.

Boice, James Montgomery. 1986. *Foundations of the Christian Faith*. Revised ed. Dover Grove, IL: Inter Varsity Press.

Capodanno, Judith, ed. 2003. *Saintly Advice: A Prayer for Every Problem*. Kansas City, MO: The Philip Lief Group, Inc.

Catechism of the Catholic Church. 2nd ed. 1997. Washington, DC: United States Catholic Conference, Inc – Libreria Editrice Vaticana.

Chesterton, G.K. 2008. *St. Francis of Assisi*. Mineola, NY: Dover Publications, Inc.

Clarke, John. 1996. *Story of A Soul: The Autobiography of Saint Thérèse of Lisieux.* 3rd ed. Washington, DC: ICS Publications.

Cooper, Kate. 2013. *Band of Angels: The Forgotten World of Early Christian Women.* New York: The Overlook Press.

Cope, Stephen. 2012. *The Great Work of Your Life.* New York: Bantam Books.

Costa, Giuseppe, ed. 2014. *Jorge Mario Bergoglio Pope Francis Thoughts and Words for the Soul.* New York: Sterling Publishing Company, Inc.

Covey, Stephen R. 1989. *The Seven Habits of Highly Effective People.* New York: Free Press.

Del Mastro, M.L. 2004. *All the Women of the Bible.* New York: Castle Books.

Edwards, Jonathan. 2015. *Sermons of Jonathan Edwards.* Peabody, MA: Hendrickson Publishers Marketing, LLC.

Englebert, Omer. 1994. *The Lives of the Saints.* Translated by Christopher and Anne Fremantle. New York: Barnes & Noble Books.

Freeman, Charles. 2009. *A New History of Early Christianity.* New Haven And London: Yale University Press.

God's Word (KJV). n.d.. Asheville, NC: Global Bible Society.

Graham, Billy. 1984. *Just As I Am: The Autobiography of Billy Graham.* New York: HarperCollins Publishers.

Graham, Billy. 1988. *The Holy Spirit.* Nashville, TN: Thomas Nelson, Inc.

Gruden, Wayne. 1994. *Systematic Theology: An Introduction to Biblical Doctrine.* Grand Rapids, MI: Zondervan Publishing House.

Halley, Henry H. 2007. *Halley's Bible Handbook.* Grand Rapids, MI: Zondervan Publishing House.

Hann, Scott, ed. 2009. *Catholic Bible Dictionary.* New York: Doubleday.

Hornsby, Sarah. 1983. *At the Name of Jesus: 365 Meditations on the Names of Jesus.* Old Tappan, NJ: Chosen Books.

Horton, David, ed. 2006. *The Portable Seminary.* Bloomington, MN: Bethany House Publishers.

Ivereigh, Austen. 2014. *The Great Reformer.* New York: Henry Holt & Company, LLC.

Kennedy, David M. 1999. *Freedom From Fear: The American People in Depression and War, 1929–1945.* New York: Oxford University Press.

Knowles, Andrew. 1993. *Discovering Prayer.* Oxford, England: Lion Publishing.

Kushner, Harold S. 1981. *When Bad Things Happen To Good People.* New York: Avon Books.

Life Application Study Bible (NIV). 1991. Wheaton, IL: Tyndale House Publishers, Inc.

Luther, Martin. 2007. *Reading the Psalms with Luther.* St. Louis, MO: Concordia Publishing House.

MacDonald, William. 1995. *Believer's Bible Commentary.* Nashville, TN: Thomas Nelson Publishers, Inc.

McGinn, Bernard. 2006. *The Essential Writings of Christian Mysticism*. New York: The Modern Library.

McGovern, Una, ed. 2005. *Dictionary of Quotations*. Edinburgh: Chambers Harrap Publishers Ltd.

McInery, Ralph, ed. 1998. *Thomas Aquinas Selected Writings*. London: Penguin Books Ltd.

Megan, Don. 2005. *Meditations with Teresa of Avila*. Novato, CA: New World Library.

Omartian, Stormie. 2010. *The Power of a Praying Life*. Eugene, OR: Harvest House Publishers.

Pelikan, Jaroslav, ed. 1990. *The World Treasury of Modern Religious Thought* (1st. ed.). Boston: Little, Brown & Company.

Pope Francis. 1989. *Open Mind, Faithful Heart*. Translated in 2013. New York: The Crossroad Publishing Company.

Pope Francis. 2013. *The Joy of the Gospel,* 1st. ed. New York: Image.

Pope Francis. 2014. *The Church of Mercy*. Chicago: Loyola Press.

Roy, Alene Adele. 1992. *In His Gardens*. Bend, OR: Maverick Publications, Inc.

Roy, Alene Adele. 1995. *Winter in His Garden*. Scappoose, OR: Closer Walk Enterprises.

Saint Augustine. 1961. *The Confessions of Saint Augustine*. Translated by Edward B. Pusey. New York: Collier Books.

Saint Augustine. 1978. *The City of God*. Translated by Marcus Dods. New York: Random House, Inc.

Salvi, Spe. 2008. *Pope Benedict XVI Saved In Hope*. San Francisco: Ignatius Press.

Schumacher, E.F. 1999. *Small is Beautiful*. Vancouver, BC: Hartley & Marks Publishing Inc.

Stamwitz, Alicia Von, ed. 2015. *The Spirit of St. Francis: Inspiring Words from Pope Francis*. Cincinnati, OH: Francisan Media.

Stanley, Charles F. 2008. *Handbook for Christian Living: Biblical Answers to Life's Tough Questions*. Nashville, TN: Thomas Nelson, Inc.

Taylor, Terry Lynn, and Mary Beth Crain. 1994. *Angel Wisdom*. New York: Harper Collins Publishers, Inc.

The Go-Anywhere Thinline Bible with the Apocrypha (NRSV). 2010. New York: HarperCollins Publishers.

Warren, Rick. 2002. *The Purpose Driven Life: What on Earth Am I Here for?* Grand Rapids, MI: Zondervan Publishing House.

Watkins, Eric, ed. 2013. *The Divine Order, the Human Order, and the Order of Nature*. New York: Oxford University Press.

Young, Sarah. 2004. *Jesus Calling: Enjoying Peace in His Presence*. Nashville, TN: Thomas Nelson.

About the Author

GUYANESE-BORN ERWIN K. Thomas, PhD, was the eldest of eleven children. Before retiring to Virginia Beach, he taught at Norfolk State University, Virginia, SUNY-Oswego, and the University of Wisconsin–Milwaukee. His undergraduate and graduate work were at the University of Oregon, Eugene, CUNY–Brooklyn, and the School of Journalism, University of Missouri–Columbia. He has published three books, the latest on the *Mass Media 2025* was by Greenwood Press (2001), and co-edited with Brown H. Carpenter. He is married to Mary Barta Thomas, and their son Matthew, with his wife, Shannon, live in Charlottesville, Virginia. In 2010, he served as vice president of the Institute for Learning in Retirement (ILR) at Old Dominion University, Virginia, and is presently a member of the Association for Education in Journalism and Mass Communication (AEJMC) Religion & Media Interest Group. He and his wife attend the Church of the Holy Apostles, – an ecumenical community of Episcopalians and Roman Catholics in Virginia Beach.

Made in the USA
Charleston, SC
17 December 2015